101 UPRIGHT BASS

STUFF ALL THE PROS KNOW AN...

BY ANDY MCKEE

Interior photos: Jeff Karp

To access audio visit:
www.halleonard.com/mylibrary

Enter Code
3143-0142-0276-2862

ISBN 978-1-4768-1278-6

HAL•LEONARD®
CORPORATION

7777 W. BLUEMOUND RD. P.O. BOX 13819 MILWAUKEE, WI 53213

In Australia Contact:
Hal Leonard Australia Pty. Ltd.
4 Lentara Court
Cheltenham, Victoria, 3192 Australia
Email: ausadmin@halleonard.com.au

Visit Hal Leonard Online at
www.halleonard.com

THE AUDIO

ABOUT THE AUTHOR

Whether you are talking about Andy McKee's bass playing or his way of moving through life, three words say it: strength, passion and artistry. Performing on the world's jazz stages for more than twenty-five years, his reputation stretches from his home base of New York, across the United States, to Europe, Japan and beyond. The deep resonance of Andy's sound adds unmistakable dimension to every band he joins. His impeccable time, musicianship and capacity for rhythmic invention were forged over years of real-world experience with legendary jazz masters. He has enjoyed extended associations with the Mingus Big Band and the Mingus Dynasty as well as groups led by Elvin Jones, Michel Petrucciani, Chet Baker, and Philly Joe Jones. He has toured and recorded as a leader of his own groups since 1995. Video clips attesting to his life on the road regularly surface on YouTube.

Throughout his career as a performing artist, Andy has enthusiastically passed on the skills and insights gained through years of study both on and off the bandstand. He has been a faculty member at The New School University in New York City since 1993 and has conducted clinics, workshops, and private lessons throughout the United States and Europe.

With his most recent publication, *101 Upright Bass Tips*, this long-time performer and educator shares his wealth of experience and knowledge with the evolving student of the upright bass. In this detailed and practical guide, you will find advice on everything from buying an instrument and strings to practice strategies, technical studies, soloing concepts, and historical notes. Enjoy!

TABLE OF CONTENTS

Tip		Page
1	Parts of the Bass	6
2	A Good Luthier Is Your Best Friend	7
3	Buying an Upright Bass	7
4	Finding the Right Strings	8
5	Changing Strings	8
6	String Height	9
7	Get a Wheel	10
8	Shoulder Strap	10
9	Rentals	10
10	Rosin	10
11	Three Sessions a Day	11
12	Good Hand Position	12
13	Balance	13
14	Simple Pizzicato Studies	14
15	3rds Studies	15
16	3rds Again	16
17	Still More 3rds	17
18	4ths Studies	18
19	Monster 5ths	19
20	Melodious 6ths	19
21	Angular 7ths	20
22	Major Scale Fingerings	21
23	Arpeggios	22
24	Arpeggios Within	23
25	Step Outside of Your Comfort Zone	24
26	Melodic Minor Scales	24
27	Set Some Limits	25
28	Fingering Options	25
29	Hammer-ons and Pull-offs	26
30	Chromatic Scales	27
31	Use a Metronome	27
32	Octave Studies	28
33	Scales with Dynamics	29
34	Warm-Up Exercise	29
35	C Major Study	30
36	Set Goals	31
37	Shifting Study	32
38	Sit or Stand	33
39	Diminished Ideas	33
40	Thumb Position Fingerings	34
41	Thumb Position Fingering Options	35
42	Thumb Position Glissando	36
43	Vibrato	36
44	Tremolo	37
45	Trills	37
46	Whole-Tone Scales	38
47	Get a Grip	39
48	Think Weight	40
49	Long Tones	40

Tip		Page
50	Note Decay	41
51	Arco Slur Studies	41
52	Think Like a Horn Player	43
53	Cross-String Exercises	43
54	Concentrate on Tempo	44
55	Half-Step Approach	45
56	Listen to Many Styles	46
57	Repeat as Needed	46
58	Sight Reading	47
59	Slap That Bass	47
60	Find the Sweet Spot	47
61	To Play or Not to Play	48
62	The "Wide Beat"	48
63	Who's Your Drummer?	49
64	Advanced Palette	49
65	Blues Roots	49
66	Functional Ear Training	51
67	Think "Relative" Harmony	51
68	Transcribe Bass Lines	52
69	Transcribe Tunes	53
70	Tritone Substitutions	53
71	V–I Studies	54
72	Adjusting the Bridge	55
73	Bridge Alignment	56
74	Car Talk	58
75	Humidifiers	58
76	Keep It Clean	58
77	Stand the Bass in the Corner	59
78	What's That Sound?	60
79	Be Concise	60
80	Breathe	61
81	Comp for Me	61
82	Don't Play on One	61
83	Don't Play the Root	62
84	Learn the Melody	62
85	Learn Lyrics	63
86	Think "Motif" in Your Solo	63
87	Rhythmic Variation	64
88	In Time/Out of Time	65
89	Up-Tempo Solos	65
90	Amp Up	66
91	Teach What You Know	66
92	Save Your Back	66
93	Memorizing Repertoire	67
94	First Rehearsal with a New Band	67
95	Play Every Chance You Get	68
96	Travel Tips	68
97	Posture	69
98	Protect Your Investment	70
99	Put on the Gloves	71
100	Did You Know?	71
101	Play the Blues	72

1 *PARTS OF THE BASS*

Your instrument is made up of many parts coming in all shapes and sizes. This diagram shows the names of the parts as they are referred to in other tips. It's especially important to be familiar with all the parts of your bass when adjustments and repairs are needed.

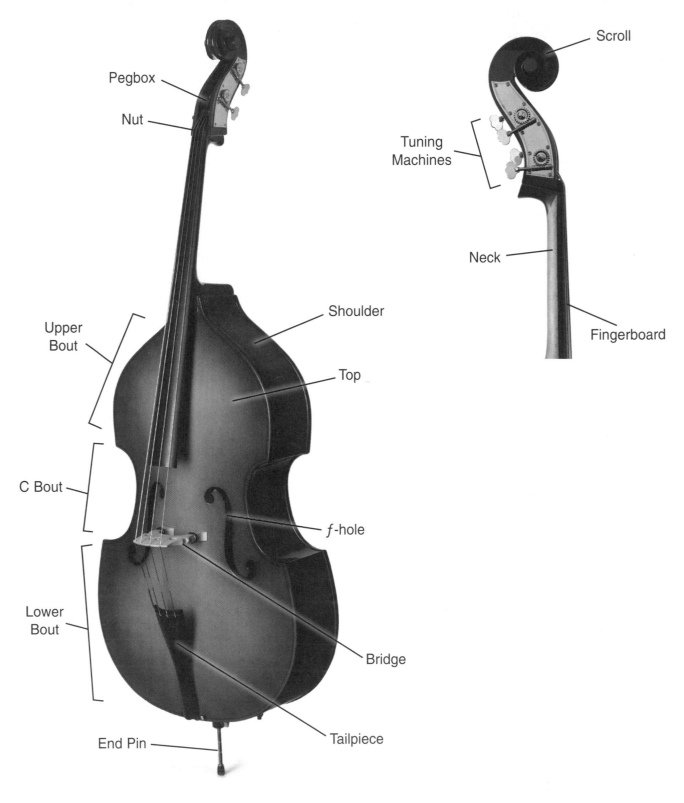

Pegbox

Nut

Scroll

Tuning Machines

Neck

Fingerboard

Shoulder

Upper Bout

Top

C Bout

f-hole

Lower Bout

Bridge

End Pin

Tailpiece

2 A GOOD LUTHIER IS YOUR BEST FRIEND

A luthier is a person who builds and/or repairs stringed musical instruments. Your bass is a remarkable assembly of wood, string, and a few bits of metal. The exact details of every dimension, joint, and angle are all very precise and serve a very specific function. A good luthier has been trained to understand these details of the instrument with the same commitment and passion as you put into learning to play it. Find a luthier to keep your bass in top playing condition. This includes everything from simple adjustments of the bridge and sound post to more complicated procedures of planing the fingerboard, fixing cracks, and gluing open seams. It's worth paying an expert to make critical repairs.

When you're traveling, make a point of finding a good luthier wherever you go. There are valuable online resources with very explicit information about the location of shops around the globe. Don't leave home without some idea of who you can turn to in the event an emergency repair is needed.

3 BUYING AN UPRIGHT BASS

Here are some things to think about when you're in the market for a bass.

- Find a good shop that deals in only string instruments, or even better, a luthier that deals in only upright basses. These places offer a much greater selection than your local music store.

- Think of your bass as an investment. If you pay a fair price today, you'll likely recapture that amount the day you decide to sell your instrument. It's possible that the value of your bass will even increase over time, so your investment may pay a dividend.

- Understand that most basses are "used." This can be a very good thing. Many of the best instruments in the world are more than 200 years old. Don't go shopping for a bass with a high luster finish in mind. While there are many fine new instruments on the market, age is by no means a reliable indication of quality or value.

- Listen. Ultimately, the most important aspect of your search is the sound of the bass. Look for an instrument that produces an even sound across all registers. It's important that all notes have a uniform character, evenness of sound, and balanced overtone distribution.

- Take your time. If you're ready to shell out the price of even an entry-level upright bass, you need to be patient. Play many different basses to get a sense of what you like in an instrument. There is a wide range of shape, body size, weight, and sound that must be considered when choosing a bass. Look for one that fits your physique and feels comfortable when you play it. Try instruments that are above and below your price range to be sure you're getting a good value for your money.

- When you think you've found the upright bass that's right for you, make an arrangement with the seller for a trial run. Take the bass home for a week and give it a good workout. Organize a rehearsal so you can hear how it sounds in an ensemble setting. Ask your instructor to check it out. If the bass stands up to these tests, you've found a winner.

4 FINDING THE RIGHT STRINGS

Sometimes having too many choices can be a problem. This is especially true when it comes to an expensive necessity like strings. Even if you've been playing the upright bass for a while, it can still be a daunting task deciding which strings are right for you. There are many to choose from, and the significant cost warrants thoughtful investigation. Consider these different qualities the next time you're on the hunt for new strings:

- **Pitch**: Is the string stable once it's in tune, or is it prone to changes in pitch?

- **Durability**: Is the string resistant to changes in humidity and temperature?

- **Tension**: Are the strings soft and easy to play, or are they tight with higher tension and a quick response?

- **Feel**: How does the string feel under your fingers? Is the surface of the string smooth or uneven and rough?

- **Balance**: Does each string in the set produce a uniform quality of sound across all registers?

- **Warm/bright**: Does the string emphasize either end of the frequency spectrum?

- **Sustain**: Is a note's decay gradual, or is the attack strong and the decay quick?

- **Pizzicato/arco**: Does the string respond differently to pizzicato and arco playing?

- **Response**: Do different dynamic levels affect the string's response?

Take time to listen closely to these attributes. Remember that every bass is different, and a string that sounds great on another bass may not sound so great on yours. Experiment with different makes and models until you find the string that's right for you and your bass.

5 CHANGING STRINGS

There are a few things to think about if you don't have much experience changing the strings on your bass. The acoustic bass is a marvel of physics. There are no screws or nails or other metal plates to hold all the pieces in place—only wood and glue and a brilliant design that puts tension in just the right places. The tension of the strings holds the bridge in place, and the pressure of the bridge on the top holds the sound post in place. The sound post is a wooden dowel carefully positioned just below the foot of the bridge (G string side) and is critical to transferring the vibration of the strings from the top to the back of the bass. The tension of the strings also keeps the nut in place.

To keep all these parts stable, it's important to change strings one at a time! With the three remaining strings still holding tension, the bridge, nut, and sound post will not move, and the delicate set-up of the instrument will remain intact.

- Start by loosening the G string until the end can be pulled through the hole in the tuning peg. Then pull the string through the hole in the tail piece, taking care that the loose end does not scratch the top.

- Carefully feed the new string through the hole in the tail piece from back to front, over the bridge and through the hole in the tuning peg. Use pencil lead to "lubricate" the groove in the bridge so the string slides easily past the contact point. The depth of this groove should be approximately one half the diameter of the string.

- For more flexible strings, try twisting the string around itself to create a firm lock once the tuning peg begins to turn **[Fig. 1]**.

- Turn the tuning machine to tighten the string, and guide the winding towards the outside of the tuning box as it wraps around the peg. To save time and strain on your wrist, get a string winder to make this job easier. As the string becomes taut, be sure it is properly aligned with the bridge and the nut. Tighten the string until it's properly tuned **[Fig. 2]**.

- Be sure the bridge does not lean toward the fingerboard as you tighten the strings. This can happen when the string does not slide smoothly over the bridge. If you notice this change, tap lightly on the top of the bridge until it is perpendicular to the top.

- Continue with the other strings, one at a time. Check to see that the bridge remains upright after tightening each string.

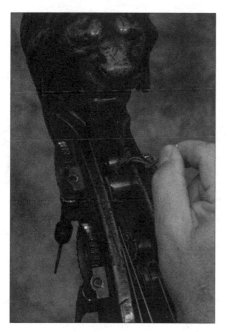

Fig. 1

Fig. 2

6 STRING HEIGHT

The height of the strings on your bass is certain to be a topic of discussion from time to time. There is no right or wrong here; it's strictly a matter of personal preference. There are some important factors to consider, however. If you're a beginner, it's best to keep the string height (or "action") fairly low to make playing easier. This will allow you to sustain longer practice sessions while gaining strength in the very specialized muscles that are used to play the bass. There's one catch; with low action on the bass, there will be some loss of volume and projection. You will probably find it necessary to use an amp in most playing situations.

Experiment with raising the strings as your strength and articulation develop. Do this in small increments so there's no noticeable strain on your left hand and arm. With the rise in string height, you'll notice an increase in sound and projection and a minimal decrease in sustain or "growl." The increased tension on the strings will deliver a stronger attack and produce greater resonance in the instrument as well as an increase in dynamic range. You may even find that there are playing situations where the amp is no longer needed.

7 GET A WHEEL

As you certainly know by now, the upright bass is a large and cumbersome instrument to haul around. A good soft bass case will have several strategically placed handles that make picking up and carrying the instrument easier, but it's still a challenge. So unless you have a chauffeur to drop you off at the door of every rehearsal and gig you'll ever have, get yourself a wheel. There are several on the market that fit in the endpin and others that attach to the outside of the case. Whichever you choose, they all work well and help to relieve stress on your body when transporting your bass.

8 SHOULDER STRAP

Wondering about other options for getting around with your bass? Think about exercising the shoulder strap option to carry your instrument like an oversized shoulder bag. Most soft cases have rings located on the sides where a shoulder strap can be attached. With this simple device, the weight of the bass is supported by your upper body, relieving stress on your lower back. Using a shoulder strap also leaves your hands free to carry other things or to grab a handrail on the stairs.

9 RENTALS

At some point in your bass playing career, it may be necessary to rent an instrument. As air travel with a bass has become increasingly difficult, there is a growing need for instruments on site. Most venues understand that the bassists on their program will be arriving without an instrument and have arrangements with local backline companies to provide one. If the venue does not provide an instrument, a short-term rental may be the only option. Check out websites like Bob Gollihur's Luthier Project where you'll find an extensive list of luthiers around the world who should be happy to help. Bass-focused websites like TalkBass.com and DoubleBassChat.com provide further valuable resources for your inquiries.

10 ROSIN

If you're going to play the upright bass, you must learn to use a bow. And if you're going to use a bow, you need to use rosin. This hardened plant extract will make the difference between a bow that produces a clear, focused sound as it grabs the string and a bow that slips past the string in silence.

Read up a bit on rosin. There are different formulas designed for different types of playing and variations in climate; harder rosins are for hot humid climates, and softer rosins are for cooler climates. Fortunately, this essential accessory is inexpensive, so your search for the perfect rosin will cost no more than a new bow tie.

Before each practice session and performance, apply rosin sparingly to the bow hair until it is slightly tacky. A good rosin should last through one hour of practice but may need to be reapplied if the bow begins to slip on the strings. Be careful not to overdo it as rosin can become caked on the bow hair, requiring a trip to the luthier for costly hair replacement. Just as you wouldn't leave your bass in a locked car, don't leave your bow in the car either. Besides the obvious security concern, excessive heat can cause the rosin to melt into the bow hair and make it hard and glassy. This too will require the attention of a professional luthier. To protect against damage to the varnished finish of the bow stick and the top of your bass, wipe away any trace of rosin dust after each playing session.

TIPS 11 – 46 : PRACTICE AND TECHNIQUE

11 THREE SESSIONS A DAY

Whether you've been playing for years or are just starting out, be sure to practice *every* day. That means seven days each week. You'll make more substantial and steady progress if your hands are on the instrument just 20 minutes daily than if you wait until Saturday and try to practice for three hours.

As your routine becomes more consistent, try dividing your practice time into three distinct sessions, each with a specific goal. They might look something like this:

- **Session 1 - technique**: scales, intervals, pizzicato, etc.

- **Session 2 - arco skills**: classical etudes, long tones, ballad melodies, orchestral excerpts, etc.

- **Session 3 - real music**: work on the material you're playing with your group or something new that you'd like to play with your group; listen to recordings; work out fingerings for melodies and written bass lines; experiment with phrasing; work on transcriptions, etc.

As there's a limit to how productive your practice time can be, take a break when your mind starts to wander. Just be sure to come back to finish the items on your practice agenda. Organizing practice sessions makes it easier to focus your mind, sharpen your skills, and bring clarity to your immediate goals. You want to develop the habit of being ready to play the moment you pick up your bass. This will have a positive impact on your playing experience as well.

And finally, trust that your practice time is having a positive impact on your playing. From time to time, you may feel that you've reached a plateau and that all your hard work is for nothing. Don't give up! The positive effects of your practice sessions may not be evident immediately, but will likely become apparent in your playing experience over weeks, months, or even years.

12 GOOD HAND POSITION

These photos show the proper shape and placement of both left and right hands. Notice the fingers of the left hand are slightly curved above the fingerboard. The spacing between the first/ second and second/fourth fingers should be fairly constant, contracting very gradually as you move to higher positions on the fingerboard.

The right hand should be closer to the end of the fingerboard than to the joint where the neck and the body of the bass meet. Moving your hand lower towards the bridge will deliver a more focused note with more pronounced overtones and a stronger attack. Anchor your thumb on the side of the fingerboard to support your fingers as you pull the strings. Experiment with using two fingers together as well as your first and second fingers independently.

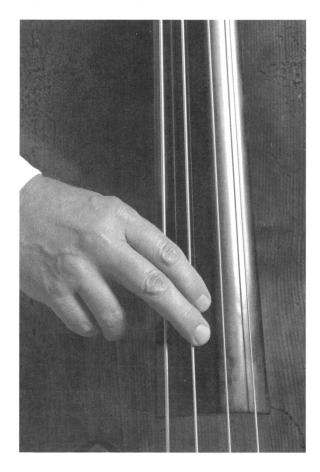

13 BALANCE

Learning to control the balance of your bass is an important issue that is often neglected. This is especially true when playing in thumb position. Place your thumb on the octave G with your fingers aligned on the string (A♭, A, B♭). Let the bass roll forward just a bit until you can feel the weight of the instrument almost falling into your fingers. Next, roll the bass back just a bit until it feels as though it's about to fall toward your left elbow. The weight of the instrument is balanced in the zone between these two points.

Work to control the weight of the instrument in this balanced position. There should be no need to rest the neck of the bass on your shoulder or to control the shoulder of the bass with your wrist. While in the balance zone, there should be no great change in your posture or your relative position with the instrument through its entire range. This understanding of balance will enable you to shift to any position with ease and continuity. You may even find the weight of the instrument can help to press the string to the fingerboard, making playing even easier and more articulate.

14 SIMPLE PIZZICATO STUDIES

Even though your right hand may seem to have a very intuitive sense about pizzicato technique, it's still worth some of your practice time. In general, the left hand faces a much greater challenge developing the techniques and articulation required to play in tune and in time. With no frets and no other visible evidence of where each note is located on the fingerboard, it's essential to work diligently over time to strengthen and refine your left-hand skills. Through all of this work, the right hand always seems to keep pace. There are, however, a few studies that are useful in bringing greater awareness to the right hand and strengthening your pizzicato technique.

In these simple studies, the object is to alternate the index and middle fingers (1, 2, 1, 2) of the right hand. Try this at first on each open string. Play the same exercise starting with your second finger and alternating 2, 1, 2, 1 as well.

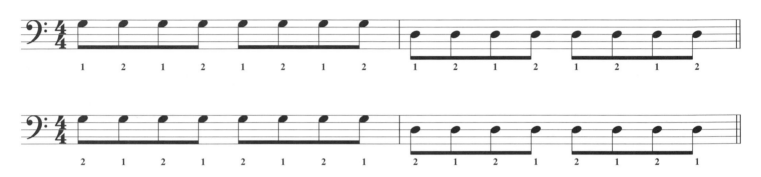

Next, try this right hand pizzicato fingering on a combination of open strings. Be disciplined with alternating only your first and second fingers. For the purpose of this study, resist the inclination to drag one finger across strings when moving from a higher to a lower string.

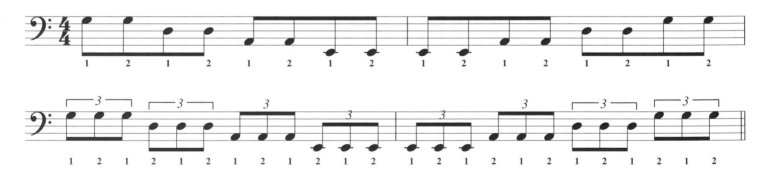

As you get your fingers under control, try playing one-octave major scales and arpeggios with the same right-hand fingering. Then move on to melodies and other studies on your music stand to see if you can maintain this disciplined pattern in your right hand, always alternating 1, 2, 1, 2 and also 2, 1, 2, 1.

15 3RDS STUDIES

The interval of a 3rd is one of the most melodic and commonly-used sounds in Western music. Everyone from Bach and Louis Armstrong to the Beatles and Rihanna use this interval in endless variation. Learn to identify the melodic quality of this sound and practice using it in your bass lines and solos.

There are numerous studies that are designed specifically to help you master fingerings for this interval. At first, practice in keys that use some open strings so that you understand the basic shape of this study and to internalize the sound of this interval. Eventually work through all keys to improve your left-hand dexterity and knowledge of the fingerboard. To keep your bow active, play through the study arco as well as pizzicato.

Here's a sequence of diatonic 3rds in B♭ major. Try this fingering, which requires playing almost the entire study in one position:

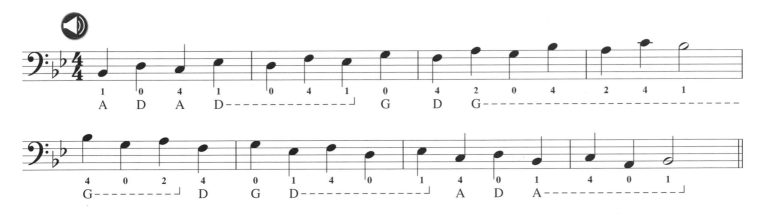

Also, practice using a fingering that moves up the fingerboard on the D string:

And try this fingering, which plays each note pair across strings:

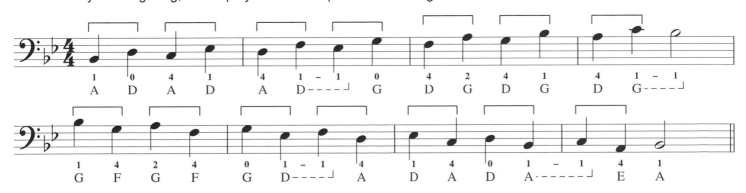

16 3RDS AGAIN

Here's a useful variation on the previous 3rds study. To improve your skills and discover applications for this sort of bass line, it's important to first internalize the sound and the technique for its execution. Adding rhythmic variation to a study not only increases the depth of understanding but improves the chances for successful application in a performance setting. You want to transform a line from a simple study into a meaningful and interesting musical phrase.

To add variation to the original study, this sequence of diatonic 3rds in B♭ is now played as a series of quarter-note triplets.

EXAMPLE 1

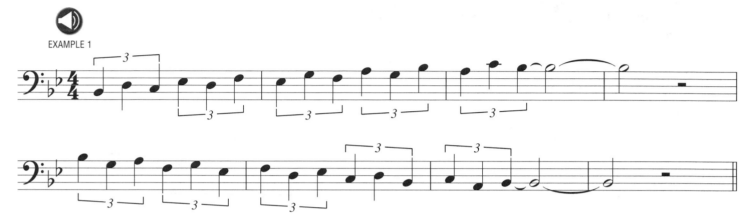

For another variation, add accents to the triplet model to create a polyrhythmic quality.

EXAMPLE 2

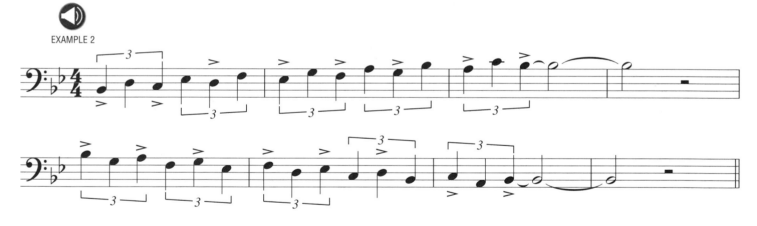

In this final rhythmic experiment, add rests to the line.

EXAMPLE 3

Play this study through all keys with both arco and pizzicato techniques.

17 STILL MORE 3RDS

Here's one more study using the interval of a 3rd. A diatonic passing tone is now included between the notes of the 3rd. Notice the very melodic quality of a line that emphasizes this interval.

EXAMPLE 1

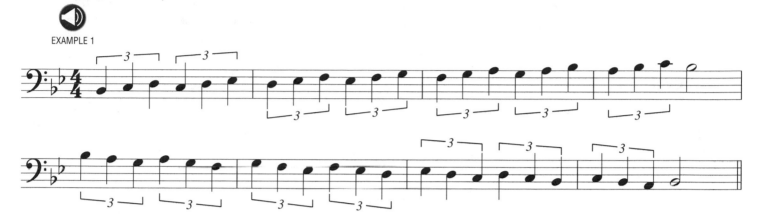

By moving this study across the bar line, a new rhythmic variation is created.

EXAMPLE 2

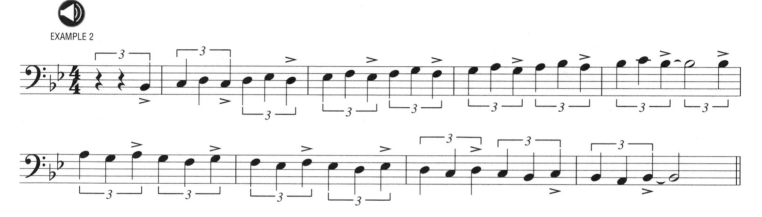

Displacing this line once again results in an even more challenging rhythmic model.

EXAMPLE 3

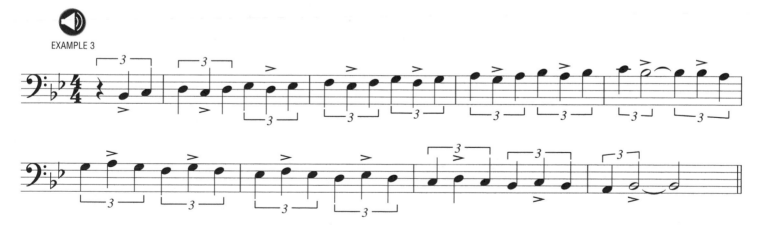

As you practice playing this study in all 12 keys, be careful to adjust your fingerings as needed. This is especially true in those keys that do not include any open strings, such as B major, D♭ major, etc. Play through this study arco as well as pizzicato.

18 4THS STUDIES

Although the 4th is one of the clearest and easiest to hear of all the intervals, playing it on the upright bass requires extra care. Here are a few fingering options that deserve a place in your practice schedule. In this first example, the fingering indicates that the 4th intervals are played by barring across strings with four notes in each position. The bracket over the staff indicates notes that are played in the same position.

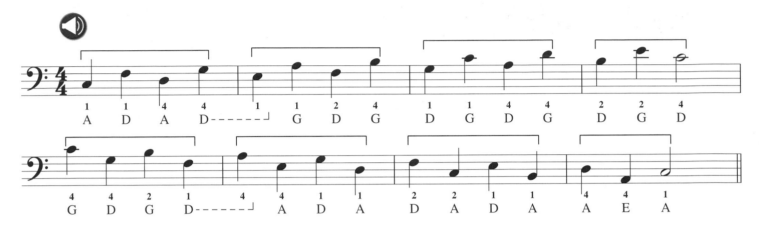

To gain more insight into fingering options for this study, try playing the series of 4ths using a triplet rhythm. With only three notes in each position, it's possible to reinforce the rhythmic basis of the line while exploring a different fingering option.

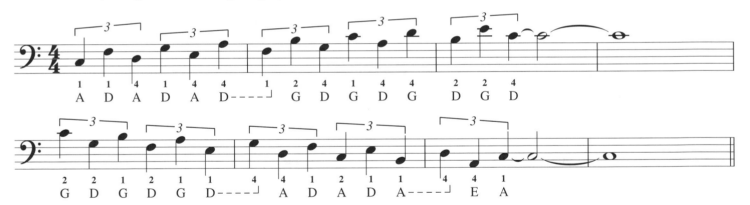

As with other studies of this sort, work through all keys and adjust fingerings as needed.

19 MONSTER 5THS

The "perfect" intervals of a 4th and a 5th are the easiest to hear and to play in tune. Here's a study to develop strength and proper hand position for playing the perfect 5th. Listen very carefully to each note pair to see that your intonation is correct before moving on to the next note pair. Try to hear even the smallest changes to your intonation as your first and fourth fingers make the necessary adjustments. This exercise is strenuous, so take your time. Play this with the bow to sustain the notes and listen closely to the sound of the perfect 5th interval.

Now play this 5ths exercise between the A and D strings and then between the E and A strings. For an even greater challenge, increase the interval between each note pair—i.e., up a minor 3rd, down a major 2nd, etc. Eventually, you could work all the way to moving up a 5th, down an augmented 4th or, for a "master" level challenge, up an octave and down a major 7th.

20 MELODIOUS 6THS

Similar to the interval of a 3rd, the 6th is one of the more mellifluous sounds in a melodic line. This interval is the distance between the first note and the sixth note of a major or minor scale. It's equal to a 5th plus either one whole step (major 6th) or one half step (minor 6th). Practice this 6ths study to better hear the interval, improve articulation playing across strings, and learn more about the location of notes on the fingerboard.

First play each 6th interval note pair across two strings and in the same position.

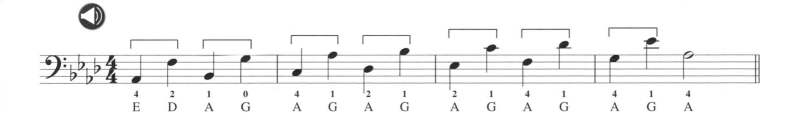

Now play the same exercise on adjacent strings with the second note of each note pair in the same position as the first note of the following pair.

Play this exercise in all 12 keys using the two fingerings described. For an additional challenge, try playing this line on just one string; i.e., shift up a 6th, then down a 5th on the same string.

21 ANGULAR 7THS

The 7th interval is more dissonant than other intervals and just a bit awkward to play on the bass. It has many useful applications, however, and is worthy of your practice time. The fingering in the first study indicates four notes are played in each position. This requires a very articulate left-hand move across strings. Remember, the bracket above the staff indicates notes that are played in the same position.

EXAMPLE 1

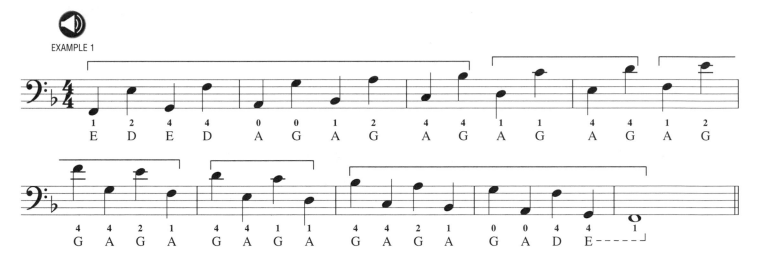

The fingering in the following study requires more shifts but may be more manageable for your left hand.

EXAMPLE 2

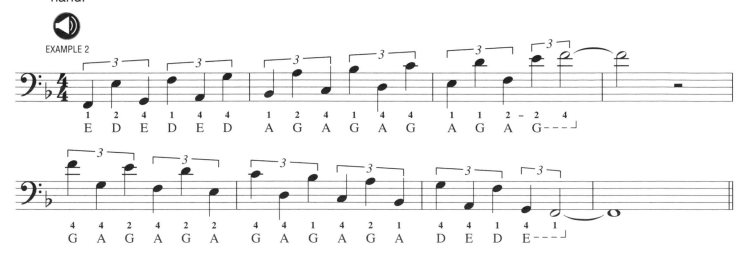

Work through this study in every key.

22 MAJOR SCALE FINGERINGS

In your efforts to develop a broader understanding of the fingerboard, it's essential to consider fingering alternatives for everything you play. As most notes on your bass can be found in two or three places on the fingerboard, it's possible to play any line in a variety of ways.

Here's a simple study to explore this important issue. First play an F major scale in two octaves, always moving immediately to the higher string across the neck to the G string. All remaining notes are then played on the G string.

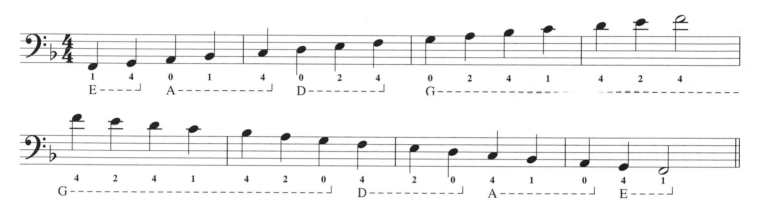

Now play the same scale adding notes to the D string.

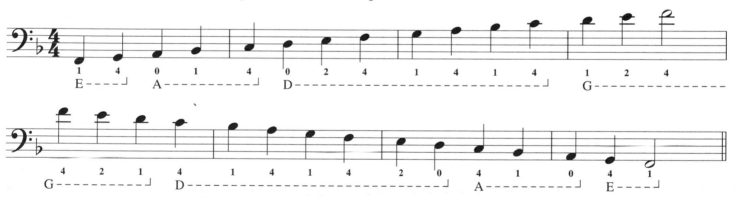

Now add notes to the A string.

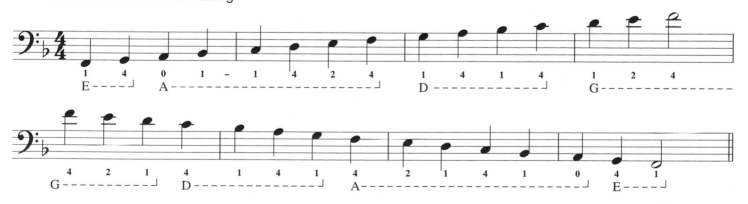

And finally, play the same scale adding notes to the E string.

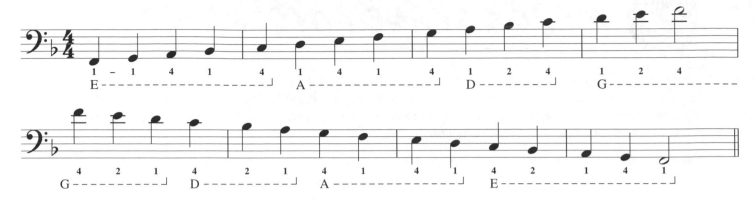

As you gain confidence with this idea, try playing in other keys using a variety of fingerings.

23 ARPEGGIOS

As you're getting major and minor scales under your fingers, remember to practice arpeggios as well. Here are the three basic chord families.

Major Seventh: Root–3rd–5th–7th

EXAMPLE 1

Dominant Seventh: Root–3rd–5th–♭7th

EXAMPLE 2

Minor Seventh: Root–♭3rd–5th–♭7th

EXAMPLE 3

Practice the three chord families in all keys, paying attention to the fingering options. This should include fingerings that play across three strings as well as just two strings, as shown here for Cmaj7.

24 ARPEGGIOS WITHIN

As you become familiar with various chords and find them easy to execute on the bass, try this study to further develop your understanding of the fingerboard and expand your harmonic perspective. When first learning about chord structure, it's normal to think of harmony from the root up: Root, 3rd, 5th, 7th, etc. Gradually, you want to explore other voicings for these chord tones. Just as a pianist plays various inversions of a chord, bassists can also affect different harmonic colors by the choice of chord tones and the order in which we play them.

Here's a study to help broaden your knowledge of harmony and improve your understanding of the fingerboard. Play this simple cycle of arpeggiated triads all within one octave. Limiting the range will force different inversions of the chords where the root tone may be the lowest, middle, or highest note in the triad.

This approach requires a certain focus, as the fingerings for the notes of each triad do not fit into any neat and repeatable pattern. Think carefully about each note's harmonic function and where it lies on the fingerboard.

Play through this study using minor triads as well. When you're ready, add the 7th to these arpeggios.

25 STEP OUTSIDE OF YOUR COMFORT ZONE

This may seem counterintuitive at first, but be sure to spend part of your practice session working on material that is not completely under your control, either because it's new or at a level of difficulty slightly beyond your skills. It's essential to work on music that's challenging and unfamiliar. Almost by definition, this material will not sound so great. How could it when it's new to your practice routine?

Recognize that important learning takes place outside of your comfort zone. Learn to resist the natural inclination to practice only material that sounds good and to dwell in the positive feedback loop that comes from playing a piece well. Sure, it's fun to imagine your neighbors enjoying all the fabulous music coming from your practice room, and that's fine. The truth is, however, that a piece sounds good because it has been on your practice schedule for some time. Develop the discipline to play through material that still doesn't sound so great. You'll be gaining new skills as you improve the musical quality of everything you play.

26 MELODIC MINOR SCALES

The melodic minor scale is quite simply a major scale with the third note lowered a half step, making the major 3rd a minor 3rd. For instance, C melodic minor would be the same as C major, except E becomes E♭.

EXAMPLE 1

Traditional music theory adds one little twist to this minor tonality by lowering the sixth and seventh notes of the scale only when descending. Still in C melodic minor, the A and B when ascending (major 6th and 7th, respectively) becomes A♭ and B♭ when descending (minor 6th and 7th, respectively).

EXAMPLE 2

This scale is used routinely for songs in minor keys, as it contains the leading tone (B) as well as the notes of the V7 (G7) chord that is so essential in basic Western harmony. Play the melodic minor scale in C to get this tonality in your ears. Then work through other keys to develop your understanding of this minor scale and other areas of the fingerboard.

F melodic minor

Bb melodic minor

27 SET SOME LIMITS

To add extra challenge to your practice, try restricting your technique in different ways. For example, scale fingerings you find in this book and other study guides usually move across strings. To add another level of difficulty, try playing a one-octave scale on just one string or a two-octave scale on just two strings. This will demand extra attention to the fingerings you choose and the shifts you make. Limiting yourself to just one string, try playing the bass line or melody of a song you're learning.

Experiment with limiting the fingers you use to play a line. This could be a study for your left or right hand. For example, play an arpeggio with only your first finger (left hand). Play a melody with only your second finger (left hand). Play a line with only your first and fourth fingers (left hand). Play a pizzicato line using only your first finger (right hand). These sorts of limitations present unique challenges and require steady focus to execute correctly.

28 FINGERING OPTIONS

String instruments have many fingering options. Almost any sequence of notes can be played several different ways: crossing strings, starting on a different string, all on one string, etc. Each particular fingering will have a slightly different sound. Learn the fingerboard well enough to comfortably play a line using several unique fingerings. Don't allow the limitations of your technique to determine how you play a line and the sound that you produce. Ultimately the musical demands of a line should determine the fingering that you choose. Your strategy should not be "I play it like this because that's the only way I can play it," but rather "I play it like this because that's how it sounds best."

To demonstrate, try playing this simple phrase on three different strings as indicated.

Listen carefully to the difference in tonal quality and describe in your mind the sound of this line on each string. Imagine how to effectively use these different qualities in your playing.

29 HAMMER-ONS AND PULL-OFFS

Hammer-ons and pull-offs are effective string instrument techniques used in all styles of music. These are essentially devices used to create slurred notes when playing pizzicato. Notes played in this way must be on the same string, unlike slurred notes with the bow, which can be played across strings.

Here's a study to strengthen your hammer-on and pull-off technique. This first example begins with hammer-ons ascending the scale and pull-offs descending.

EXAMPLE 1

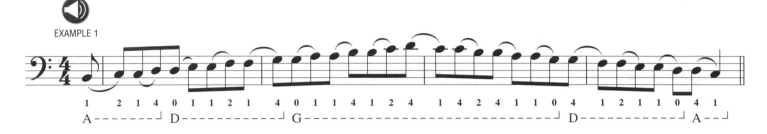

This next example is the reverse, using pull-offs ascending the scale and hammer-ons descending.

EXAMPLE 2

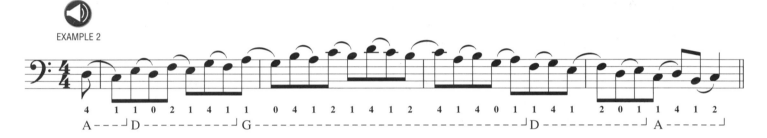

Now try this line that includes hammer-on/pull-off combinations.

EXAMPLE 3

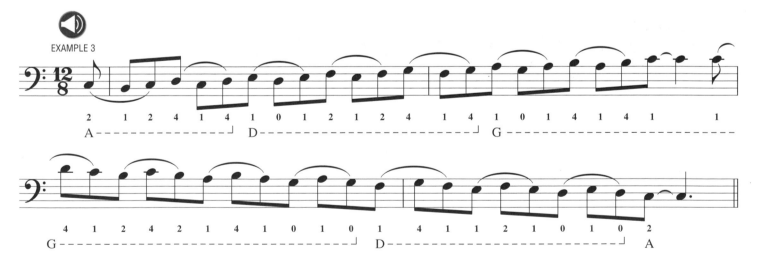

Work through these studies in all 12 keys, making adjustments to fingerings so that slurred notes are always played on the same string.

30 CHROMATIC SCALES

Probably the most challenging scale to play on a string instrument is the chromatic scale. This series of 12 consecutive half steps has a very unique sound. It's generally the least used in Western music so it is the least familiar to our ears. On a piano, this scale would include every key (black and white) between any note and one octave higher. Depending on the starting point, you'll need to adjust fingerings so that you manage to play three notes in each position and avoid shifting to the highest note. This example shows a chromatic scale starting on C with fingerings.

EXAMPLE 1

Play this scale beginning on all 12 pitches, being sure to play just one octave ascending, and then return to the starting note. Experiment with different fingerings, including those which play the entire scale on only one string, as in this example starting on the open D.

EXAMPLE 2

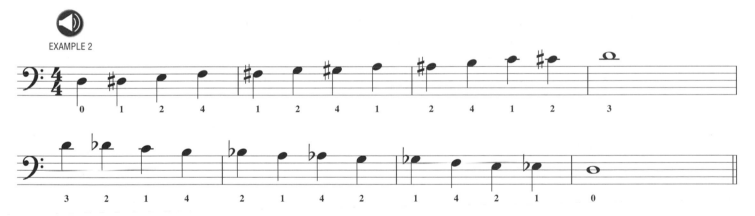

When you feel prepared for a greater challenge, add a second and even a third octave to this study.

31 USE A METRONOME

Virtually everything we play is in time. Even a rubato passage can be measured in real time and requires a sense of duration and pulse. For this reason, a metronome is an essential tool in the practice room. Use one to keep a steady pulse through everything you play—from simple scales to the most difficult material on your music stand. An internal sense of time will evolve as you practice with a metronome and gain experience playing in different situations.

Here's an experiment to keep things interesting. Once you get the notes of a new piece under your fingers, find a tempo where you can play from beginning to end without stopping (even if this is much slower than the eventual performance tempo). Play through the piece at this base tempo. Now set the metronome 3 bpm faster and play the piece from beginning to end. Then set the metronome 6 bpm slower and play the piece again. Continue playing at divergent tempos, being aware of the very different problems you encounter. Playing the line at a faster tempo may be more difficult for your left hand (shifting, crossing strings, etc.), whereas playing at a slower tempo may pose a challenge to phrasing, maintaining a steady tempo, and sustaining the proper feel of the piece. After three or four moves in either direction, return to the base tempo and notice whether the piece feels more relaxed and your playing is more confident.

32 OCTAVE STUDIES

The octave is the largest interval to be discussed in this book. The simplest fingering for this interval is across two strings—i.e., between the E and D strings or between the A and G strings. Playing a note and the octave above can be accomplished quite easily using the first finger for the low note and fourth finger for the octave.

Playing a series of octaves, however, demands a bit more planning for fingerings that are most efficient. In the example below, you'll find two different options. In the first, each octave pair is played in the same position using the first and fourth fingers. (Remember that the bracket above the staff indicates a group of notes to be played in the same position.)

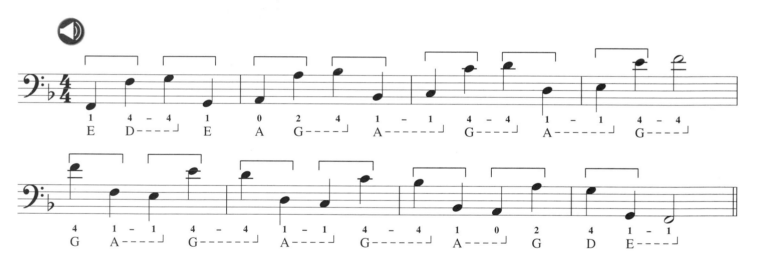

In this second option, you'll find a much more efficient fingering that includes as many as four notes in each position. This economy of motion is critical to developing a strong and articulate left-hand technique and a broader understanding of the fingerboard.

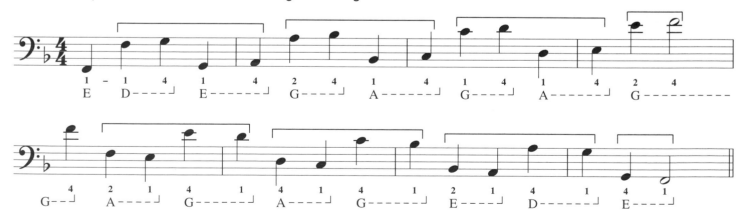

33 SCALES WITH DYNAMICS

Here's an idea to add a new challenge to your practice of basic scales. Play through a one octave scale (ascending and descending) with a gradual crescendo to the highest note and a decrescendo returning to the lowest note. Work through this study both arco and pizzicato. Listen carefully to be sure that each successive note is increasing in volume while ascending and decreasing in volume while descending.

When you feel confident and in control of this dynamic parameter, play more than just one octave: to the 3rd above, the 5th, and eventually even to the second octave. Adding notes to the ascending line will require greater control and sensitivity as the increments of increasing volume become smaller. Imagine the control you would need to play three octaves with a very even and measured crescendo/decrescendo spread over 22 notes. To keep this study interesting, try inverting the dynamic shape by playing a decrescendo while ascending and a crescendo while descending.

34 WARM-UP EXERCISE

Sometimes there's very little time to get ready for a recital or other performance, and a quick warm-up is essential to good execution starting with the first note. The exercise on the next page is meant to get the blood flowing to your fingers as you prepare for everything from performance to your daily practice session. Each measure is played as a double stop, holding one note while the note on the adjacent string changes. For example, in the first measure, hold down E on the D string (first finger) and trill B to A♯ on the G string (fourth and second fingers). Practice slowly and in time, paying close attention to your hand position and intonation. More than a simple callisthenic exercise, this study is designed to strengthen your left hand and reinforce the correct spacing between your fingers. As with any new practice, discontinue if you start to feel physical strain.

Another goal of this study is to reinforce the slightly curved shape of your fingers. For instance, in the second measure, your second and fourth fingers must arch over the G string to avoid muting the A.

EXAMPLES 1-6

When your fingers are ready, try playing this study with these bowing variations.

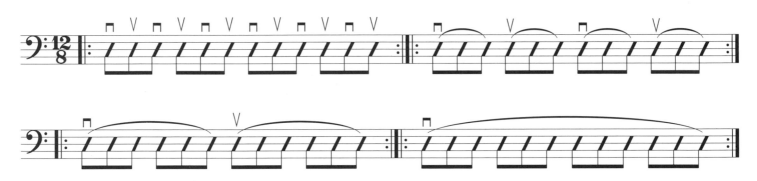

35 C MAJOR STUDY

Here's a great study to get your fingers moving and to develop a bit of rhythmic diversity in a basic eighth-note line. Work to master this piece without any slurs to build confidence in your fingerings from beginning to end. Then work through the variations on the next page that include slurs to be played both arco and pizzicato. As slurs must be played on the same string when playing pizzicato, there must be slight alterations to the fingerings you choose.

EXAMPLE 1

Variations:

36 SET GOALS

Setting goals is a strategy used by successful people in all disciplines at every level of accomplishment. This important process is an effective tool to focus your efforts on specific activities, motivate you to increase your work load (practice time), and persevere through periods that seem unproductive. Setting goals will help you to feel a greater sense of direction and purpose.

Think of goals in two distinct categories.

Short-term goals include objectives that you can accomplish today, this week, or possibly this month. Examples might include:

- Play through minor scales and arpeggios in every key.

- Play a melody up to a certain metronome setting.

- Learn a new song.

- Transcribe eight measures of the bass line from a recording you like.

Long-term goals include objectives that require sustained attention over a period of one month or more. Examples might include:

- Develop a controlled vibrato in thumb position.

- Memorize a complicated and extended melody.

- Learn the Koussevitzky concerto for double bass.

- Write a composition that features the upright bass.

- Save money for a better instrument.

Set goals that are realistic based on your current skill level and the inevitable limits of your practice time. By taking specific and calculated steps, you can measure your progress and take pride in achieving the goals you set. This will give a boost to your self-confidence as a bassist and act as a motivation to continue on in your musical pursuits.

37 SHIFTING STUDY

Most of what we play requires some amount of shifting up and down the neck. The intervals in any type of scale are all relatively small: minor 2nds, major 2nds, and sometimes a minor 3rd. This means that most basic bass lines can be played within a relatively compact area of the fingerboard. The study below emphasizes wider intervals of a 10th and requires larger shifts. Practicing these intervals will help you to develop a more fluid motion up and down the fingerboard and strengthen your transitions in and out of thumb position as well.

Starting on C, play the root tone, then the 10th (E), and then play one octave lower (E) leading to the next root tone (F). Continue through this cycle of 4ths until you return to the key of C. When necessary, play the descending interval as two octaves to avoid reaching far into thumb position (measures 2, 4, etc.). Work at a slow tempo with a focus on fluid shifts and precise intonation. Play this study both arco and pizzicato.

38 SIT OR STAND

There are great upright bass players who sit when they play and ones who stand. There is no right or wrong in this regard; it's strictly a matter of personal preference. If you're a beginner on the acoustic bass, practice both sitting and standing to determine which is more comfortable for you. A stool for this purpose should be around 30 inches high. If you're a dedicated student and practicing long hours (more than three hours daily), consider sitting for some portion of your practice time. This will relieve stress on your lower back and allow easier access to thumb position while you learn more about the balance of the instrument. Be sure to also consider which position allows you to project your musical energies most effectively.

39 DIMINISHED IDEAS

The diminished scale is a series of whole step/half step intervals that has a uniquely transitional sound. The diminished arpeggio consists of a series of minor 3rds that lay very neatly on the fingerboard of the double bass. Once you've worked through major and minor scales, add some studies of diminished scales and arpeggios to your practice routine. Even though this tonality has a limited transposition, it's useful to practice these scales and arpeggios beginning on all 12 chromatic pitches to become familiar with its sound and comfortable with its execution.

Here are two fingering ideas for the diminished scale. The ascending line shows the whole step played in one position (ex. E♭–F), and the shift moves to the note one half step higher (F–G♭). Descending, the half step interval is played in the same position (E♭–D), and the shift moves to the note one whole step lower (D–C).

EXAMPLE 1

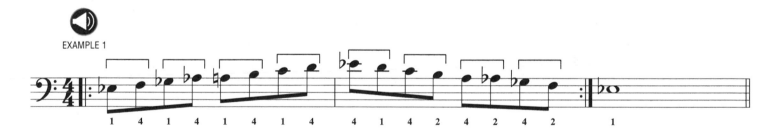

This simple fingering for the E♭ diminished arpeggio begins on the A string.

EXAMPLE 2

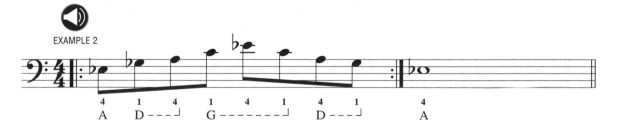

Try this study in 12/8 for a more challenging practice of diminished arpeggios.

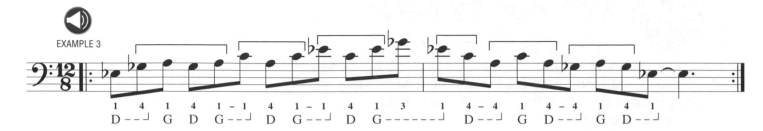

EXAMPLE 3

40 THUMB POSITION FINGERINGS

It is important to gradually explore fingering possibilities in thumb position. Your thumb is now on top of the fingerboard and used to play notes along with the first, second, and third fingers. As a good starting point, think of a series of half steps similar to the fingerings in the lower register. Anchor each position with your thumb (notated as "+") and use your fingers to play the following example.

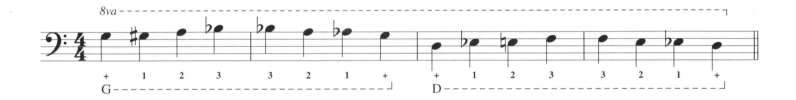

Now try moving higher on the fingerboard, playing the A♭ with your thumb and adjusting the half-step series accordingly.

Continue moving up the fingerboard in this series of half steps until your third finger reaches the D above the octave G. Be sure not to strain while experimenting in thumb position. Work to keep your left shoulder relaxed and your upper body over your hips—not hunched over the shoulder of the instrument. Be aware of your hand position, keeping your elbow slightly raised and your hand over the fingerboard.

41 THUMB POSITION FINGERING OPTIONS

As you gain confidence and balance in thumb position, consider some fingering options that will allow greater flexibility in the upper register. With the notes closer together in this region of the fingerboard, execution of larger intervals now becomes possible. In place of a series of half steps, it's entirely possible to include whole steps (or whole tones, "W.T.") within each position leading to a variety of alternatives.

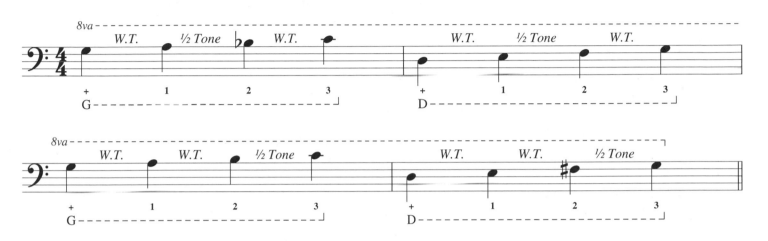

Playing the C note on the A string makes it possible to play this major scale without any shift. Be sure to anchor your hand position with your thumb on the octave D and G and play the following C major example with the indicated fingerings.

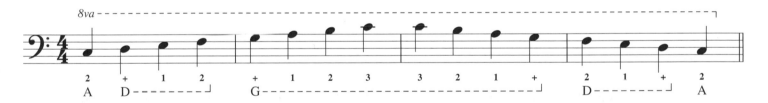

The same concept applies to any other type of scale as well. Try this C melodic minor scale, adjusting the fingerings as needed and starting on the A string as in the example above.

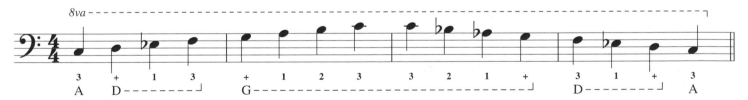

Experiment with other fingerings in thumb position using various combinations of half and whole steps within each position.

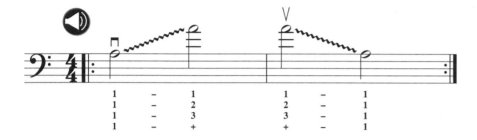 42 THUMB POSITION GLISSANDO

The transition into and out of thumb position is one of the most challenging motions to master. To access the full range of the instrument, this motion must be relaxed and fluid. Work to develop a posture that allows you to place your thumb on the strings at the octave with little adjustment to your shoulders and upper body. Strive to make this move into the upper register smooth and effortless.

Here's a simple study to help you develop a sense of balance with the instrument and an easy transition into and out of thumb position. Using the bow, play a glissando (slide from one note to the next) on the G string from the A note to one an octave higher. As the fingerings indicate, play the low A with your first finger to the octave A with your first, second, and third fingers, and even with your thumb.

Work to keep your upper body erect and your elbow above (but not touching) the shoulder of the bass. Try playing octave shifts to other notes on the G string—i.e., B♭ to B♭, B to B, and so on.

43 VIBRATO

EXAMPLES 1-2

Vibrato is a string instrument technique that brings a vocal quality to the sound of a melodic line. Some basic understanding of this sound is essential for any student of the double bass. Whether you've been playing for years or you're just a beginner, this is a good study to help gain control of this technique.

Playing whole notes with the bow, rock your finger back and forth on any note to get the feel for the motion that will produce a vibrato. Move along the line of the string—not across the fingerboard as you might with an electric guitar. Work slowly at first to control the speed and width of the very slightly changing pitch. Next, set a metronome to 80 bpm. Again, play whole notes, but work to play a very measured vibrato. Rock your finger back and forth at the speed of an eighth note, eighth-note triplet, sixteenth note, etc. Try this with each finger and work to control the speed and width of your vibrato.

Notice how your forearm, wrist, and finger are all involved in this relaxed and even motion. As you gain control in the lower register, try moving up the neck and even into thumb position. Here you'll need to work to hold your arm and hand above the fingerboard so that the motion is not restricted by clinging to the shoulder of the instrument. Again, work to control the speed and width of your vibrato so you can use it effectively in various melodic passages.

TREMOLO

The tremolo is an important musical effect that is common to string instruments and worthy of your time and practice. With the bow, tremolo is produced by rapidly alternating up and down bows on a single note. For best results, practice producing this special sound between the middle and the tip of the bow. The relaxed motion of this technique comes almost entirely from the wrist and forearm.

The notation for tremolo looks like this:

Pizzicato tremolo can be produced by rapidly repeating a note alternating between the first and second fingers of the right hand. This technique can simulate the sustained sound of a note played with the bow.

TRILLS

The trill is another important melodic ornamentation you want to learn to control. This technique requires a rapid alternation between two adjacent notes, either one whole step or one half step apart, played on the same string. A trill can be played arco using one long bow stroke or pizzicato using an assertive hammer-on/pull-off to sustain the vibration of the string.

Practice this effect slowly at first to control the speed and to maintain clear intonation. The notation for a trill looks like this:

To develop this technique, try practicing major scales adding a trill to every other note.

46 WHOLE-TONE SCALES

While most diatonic scales divide the octave into a particular sequence of whole and half steps, the whole-tone scale consists of a series of notes separated by a major 2nd (one whole step) and contains only six notes. This tonality has an unsettled, dream-like harmonic quality due to the symmetry of all chords and intervals: there are no leading tones, no perfect 5ths, no major or minor triads. Like the diminished scale, this scale is a mode of limited transposition (it can be transposed only once before an identical set of notes is repeated). To become familiar with the whole-tone sound and comfortable with its execution, play through this scale beginning on all twelve chromatic pitches.

Here's a basic fingering for the whole-tone scale starting on low F. Notice the simple repetition of the 1-4 fingering, which can be used beginning on any note and in any register.

EXAMPLE 1

Now try this sequence of augmented triads built on each degree of the whole-tone scale.

EXAMPLE 2

47 GET A GRIP

The two photos below show the proper way to hold a French-style bass bow. Drape your fingers over the bow keeping them somewhat perpendicular to the stick. Place your thumb just in front of the frog so that you are controlling the stick. Your grip on the bow should be firm yet flexible.

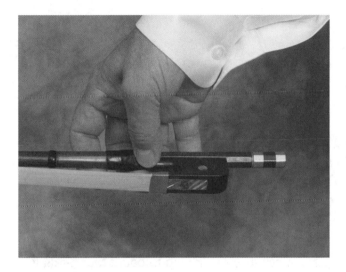 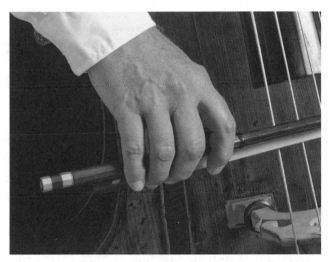

These photos show the proper way to hold a German-style bass bow. Your fingers should be slightly curved and relaxed with your thumb over the top of the stick and your little finger under the frog.

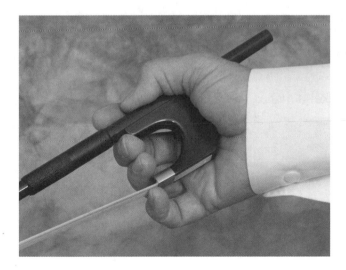 

48 THINK WEIGHT

When considering the proper language to describe arco technique, think "weight" and not "pressure" or "strength." The bow should exert a constant weight on the string and maintain contact with the string throughout the stroke. Practice long tones to isolate the bowing motion and to explore the mechanism that transfers the weight of your arm to the contact point between the bow hair and the string. Eventually, you want to sustain a note with a uniform resonance and projection from the frog to the tip and back again to the frog. This is not a matter of pressing the bow into the string but rather allowing the weight of your arm to sustain a consistent contact between the bow and the string.

49 LONG TONES

Practicing long tones can have a very positive impact on a wide range of playing issues. This study isolates the bow stroke so you can work on your grip and the motion of your arm without the complications of pitch, rhythm, string crossings, etc. There should be flexibility in your elbow and wrist so the motion is not coming from only your shoulder. Practice playing open strings with the metronome set on 40 bpm and count four beats for each note, alternating between down-bow and up-bow. Be patient and listen closely to the sound you produce at each point on the bow.

When you have mastered bow control, try playing simple scales while continuing to count four beats for each note. Listen closely to the sound when you change from down-bow to up-bow and visa versa. Aim to make this transition as imperceptible as possible with no pause in the sound you produce. As your skills become more consistent and you produce a uniform sound throughout the bow stroke, move on to five or six beats per note.

Just for fun, try this variation: play a major scale counting two beats for the tonic and adding one beat for each successive note until you reach the octave. By this method, the octave will be held for nine beats. Then play the same scale descending starting with two beats for the octave and adding one beat for each note until you return to the tonic.

Keep in mind that this study's focus is on the bow stroke: a motion that includes your fingers, hand, wrist, forearm, elbow, upper arm, and shoulder.

50 NOTE DECAY

Here is a graphic representation of a four-note line played both pizzicato and arco. Notice the strong attack and immediate decay that is typical of a note played pizzicato. Once the string is released, the vibration begins to dissipate immediately, and the decrease in volume is dramatic.

EXAMPLE 1

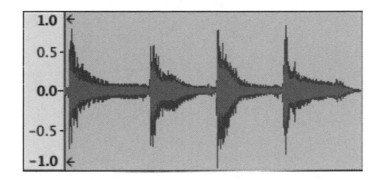

A note played arco, however, has the potential to sustain over a longer time period and even to grow in volume. You can see each note remains relatively constant in volume, up to the start of the following note.

EXAMPLE 2

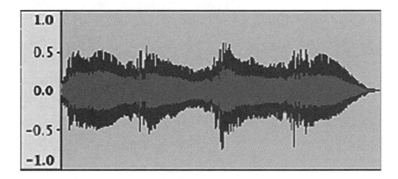

This simple principle of physics has an interesting impact on our playing, as it offers a variety of options for executing a melodic line. Experiment with playing a line both arco and pizzicato. Listen closely to the duration of each note and compare the continuity of your line. Notice that a line played pizzicato will project a more rhythmic quality, while the same line played arco will assume a more melodic and vocal quality.

51 ARCO SLUR STUDIES

Using the bow offers a wide variety of phrasing options that are not possible in a pizzicato line. Any combination of detached and slurred notes creates a unique sound that should be deliberate and specific. The quality or meaning of a line can be radically altered by choosing a different bowing combination.

Play through these studies to get the feeling of different bow strokes and how a phrase can be manipulated by slurs.

First, alternate down-bow/up-bow with no slur:

EXAMPLE 1

Next, use a slur for each triplet starting on the beat:

EXAMPLE 2

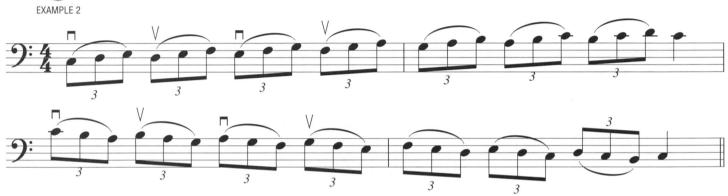

Then slur each triplet starting off the beat:

EXAMPLE 3

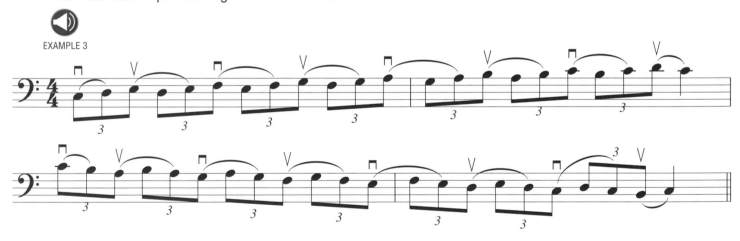

And finally, play the same phrase with a slur of two notes:

EXAMPLE 4

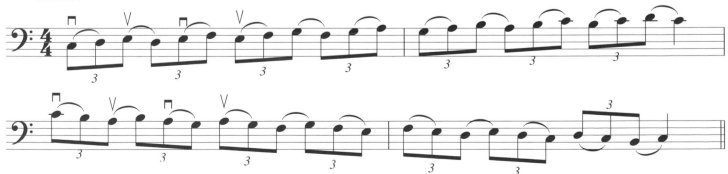

52 THINK LIKE A HORN PLAYER

If you're somewhat new to playing with the bow, it's important to think a little differently about the melodic quality of the lines you play. Pizzicato playing is characterized by a forceful attack followed by a sudden decay of the note (see tip #50). The emphasis on the attack gives a pizzicato line a very distinctive and useful rhythmic drive.

Arco playing, however, allows a note to sustain past the initial attack. With a bow, it's even possible to increase the volume of a note over time. To effectively execute a melody with the bow, it's important to think like a horn player who maintains air flow through a phrase, sustains the resonance of each note through its intended duration, and joins one note to the next with a consistent dynamic. In this way, a melodic phrase played with the bow can have a larger dynamic arc than the punctuated rhythmic quality of a pizzicato line.

In your practice, be aware of the duration of each note you play. With the bow, it's possible to sustain a note through its entire rhythmic value. A quarter note beginning on the first beat ends at the start of the second beat—not before. Perhaps more obvious, a whole note begins on the first beat and ends at the start of the next measure.

53 CROSS-STRING EXERCISES

Playing across strings with the bow is an essential skill for any serious student of the double bass. The motion should involve the wrist and forearm, with very little movement from the shoulder. The exercise below is designed to develop control and flexibility with the bow. Use a metronome to help sustain an even rhythm and use short bow strokes no matter what tempo you choose.

Play the same figure with these alternate bowings:

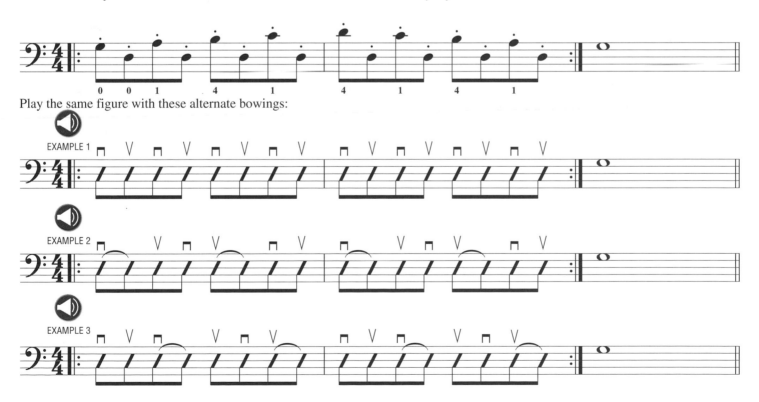

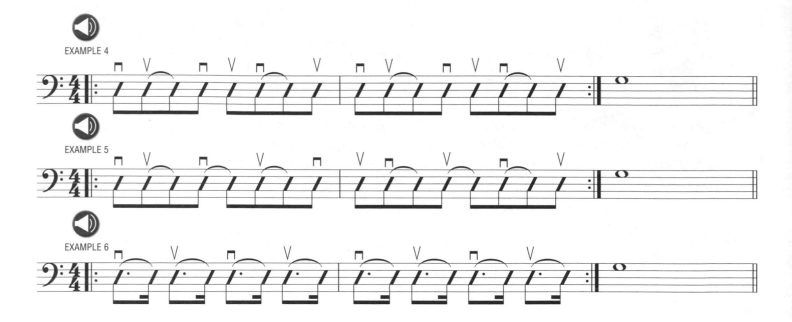

EXAMPLE 4

EXAMPLE 5

EXAMPLE 6

Try this study also across the D and A strings and the A and E strings.

TIPS 54 – 64 : BASS LINES

54 CONCENTRATE ON TEMPO

Especially in the world of bassists and drummers, there is much discussion of the "beat." Do you play "on top" of the beat? Do you play "behind" the beat? "What's up with his beat?" These are provocative questions with few clear and concise answers. More often than not, someone who plays "on top" of the beat is actually rushing the tempo—i.e., speeding up. Conversely, someone who plays "behind" the beat is actually slowing down. Both tendencies should be avoided.

Infinitely more important than where you place your notes within the beat, however, is your ability to play and project a clear and steady tempo. Concentrate on a consistent tempo and the pulse that you project. As your timing becomes more stable, your own intuitive sense of feel will evolve naturally. Elvin Jones did not think to himself, "I'll play behind the beat, and Trane will love that and give me the gig." Rather, he developed a resolute sense of pulse and was able to project an unmistakable sense of time and feel. Pundits' suggestions that Elvin played in the "middle" of the beat or "behind" the beat will always be an outsider's view. What really mattered was the clarity of pulse and an intuitive feel that made his drumming so profound.

55 HALF-STEP APPROACH

Here's a simple idea that will bring convincing results with just a bit of practice. It's common and useful to play the root of a chord on the first beat of a measure or any time the chord changes. This provides a foundation for other players in the ensemble and brings clarity to the harmonic direction of a tune. In this study, you need to think carefully about not only the root of each chord but also the approach tone: the note you play just *before* that root tone. The concept is simple: approach each root tone from a note one half step above or below the target root tone.

To demonstrate, here's an exercise where each chord lasts the duration of two beats. Play the root of each chord on beats 1 and 3 and an approach tone one half step lower than the target root tone on beats 2 and 4 through this cycle of 4ths. Notice that the register may change at any place in the line.

EXAMPLE 1

Now try the same chord sequence using an approach tone one half step above the target root tone.

EXAMPLE 2

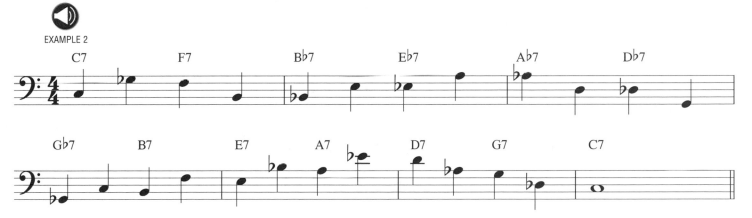

Play these lines in different positions on the fingerboard. Be inventive with the changing register and include some notes in thumb position.

When you're comfortable with this concept and able to easily execute the cycle of 4ths progression, try expanding the chords to four beats each. Continue with half-step resolutions from beat 4 to each root tone on beat 1 while filling in beats 2 and 3 with other scale or chord tones.

EXAMPLE 3

56 LISTEN TO MANY STYLES

In order to understand the universal function of the upright bass, it's important to listen to a wide range of musical styles. Listen to blues, country, jazz, classical, rock, bluegrass, show bands, and anything else that interests you. Learn to recognize a quality upright bass sound and a well-constructed bass line even if the style is not one that you imagine playing. Work to expand your appreciation for music outside your comfort zone—this will deepen your understanding of all the music you play and strengthen the effectiveness of the sound you create.

57 REPEAT AS NEEDED

Do you worry that there's something wrong when you find yourself repeating a bass line over and over? Don't sweat it! There's no harm in repeating a line as long as it's well structured and fits the musical context. This approach provides a solid foundation for the ensemble sound. Sometimes an ostinato-style line satisfies the musical demands of the situation where greater variation would be too complex and weaken the aural core. You can hear a stellar example of this approach in Steve Davis' bass line on John Coltrane's recording of "My Favorite Things." Throughout most of the fourteen-minute track, Davis plays just two notes that provide a balance to the complex rhythmic and harmonic playing by the other musicians in the ensemble.

So the next time you find yourself repeating a bass line, listen closely and trust your instincts. You just might be providing the perfect center around which your bandmates can solo, groove, etc. Move gradually away from your ostinato line when, in your ear, the musical context demands greater variation.

58 SIGHT READING

Like most skills, sight reading improves only by doing it. Read everything you can get your hands on. Read big band charts, classical etudes, lead sheets, and trombone chorales. Read James Jamerson bass lines and music for bassoon. Read *everything*.

Make sight reading a part of your daily practice routine. This means finding books full of music, starting at the beginning, and playing through to the end. Be sure to find material that's challenging yet approachable. Try reading a piece at different tempos. At a faster tempo, you may have to count through certain measures just to keep the piece moving forward. At a slower tempo, work to execute the piece with rhythmic precision, accurate intonation, a full sound, and correct bowings.

In a live performance setting, there are some things to keep in mind. Before the downbeat, look for these important signs: key signature and key changes, time signature and time signature changes, fast sequences of notes, syncopations, repeat signs, and the coda. Make a mental note of these important features of the piece and think through rhythms and fingerings for the most difficult passages. With these ideas in mind, you'll have a better chance of reading the music as written and getting a call back. (See tip #61, "To Play or Not to Play.")

59 SLAP THAT BASS

For an excursion into bass history, check out the sound and technique of slapping the bass. For nearly 100 years, this percussive sound has been central to various genres of popular music around the world. From Pops Foster playing in early Dixieland bands to rockabilly, punkabilly, and country players of today, slapping the bass has added a unique character and rhythmic drive to the sound of the instrument.

Long before the acoustic bass could benefit from the electronic inventions of the microphone and the transducer style pick-up, string height was maximized to help project the sound of the instrument. With high action, pulling the string away from the instrument and allowing it to snap back against the fingerboard adds a percussive element to the bass note typically played on beats 1 and 3. Between these notes, on beats 2 and 4, the right hand slaps the strings against the fingerboard to sustain the rhythmic drive of the bass line. To learn more about the sound and feel of slapping the bass, listen to both early and current recordings of bass players who employ this special technique like Willie Dixon, Bill Black, and Lee Rocker.

60 FIND THE SWEET SPOT

There will certainly come a time that you have to play an unfamiliar instrument in a rehearsal or gig. When this occasion arises, take the time to carefully assess the instrument prior to playing to find its strengths and weaknesses. This may include variations in volume from one string to the other, variations in timbre from one note to another, unfamiliar string length, uncomfortable string height (too high or too low), awkward endpin adjustment, unfamiliar size or shape of the instrument, and other peculiarities.

Play a few warm-up studies or excerpts from the music you're about to perform to get a sense of how the instrument is going to respond. If there are notes that are weak on one string but stronger on another, or a particular register that is weak, make a mental note and plan to recalculate your fingerings to accommodate the vagaries of the instrument du jour. Focus on the good qualities of the bass and exploit the notes that respond and project the best.

61 TO PLAY OR NOT TO PLAY

When you're reading through a new arrangement with your favorite big band, you naturally want to sound your best and play the part perfectly. There's great satisfaction in reading well and executing difficult passages that are locked in with other instruments. At the same time, there's also wisdom in knowing when to just lay out. No matter how well you sight-read, there will inevitably come a passage that is beyond your skill level. When that moment arrives, it's best to count carefully through that difficult measure or two and get back to playing as soon as you feel confident. You won't lose the gig because you can't sight-read a passage that everyone in the band knows is very difficult. On the other hand, you might lose the gig if you play a passage very poorly, get lost as a result, and have to stop the rehearsal to find your place before going on.

And don't forget to do your homework. When the rehearsal is over, be certain to get a copy of that difficult passage and practice it at home. Then you'll be ready to nail it at the next rehearsal.

62 THE "WIDE BEAT"

In jazz, there is often reference to a "wide beat"—a certain relaxed rhythmic quality associated with an authentic "straight ahead" swing groove. Detailed analyses of how master jazz musicians subdivide the beat into eighth notes reveal a ratio somewhere around 44:1. That is to say, it's a bit longer than the standard triplet interpretation of an eighth note (33:1) but not evenly dividing the beat in half (50:1). Keep in mind that this number is only an average and should be understood as a mathematical representation of a "wide beat."

To gain some understanding of this rhythmic dynamic, practice playing an eighth-note line with a very precise triplet interpretation. Next, play the same line with a very precise even-eighth interpretation. Then work to play the line with a rhythmic quality somewhere between the two. This requires as much acute listening as it does articulate execution of the line. Over time, your playing will reflect not one or the other but a dynamic range, moving purposefully between the poles of a very triplet-oriented rhythmic quality and a nearly even-eighth quality depending on the melodic demands of a particular line and your own musical sensibilities.

63 WHO'S YOUR DRUMMER?

The intuitive connection between you and your drummer defines the basis of the rhythm section and the foundation of an ensemble's sound. Establishing this connection should be your primary concern when playing in a new band. First listen to the kick drum; it's the aural foundation of the overall drum kit and occupies a frequency range that intersects with your bass. Learn to quickly assess the drummer's sense of the pulse and feel and make adjustments to your own sense of these things. Remember that it is through a collective effort that we project a clear sense of time and feel.

Like any successful relationship, there must be a large measure of trust between partners. If the drummer plays a fill that is not exactly in time, can you trust that you will be together on beat 1 of the next measure? If you take some rhythmic risks in the bass line, can you depend on your drummer to hold down the groove and set you up for re-entry? As you and your drummer cultivate a sense of trust, you strengthen the rhythmic stability and depth of feel for the entire ensemble. The willingness to build a solid connection between you and your drummer is essential to attain higher levels of musical achievement and a sign of a confident and mature musician.

64 ADVANCED PALETTE

Listening to creative bassists of the past fifty years, you'll surely encounter some sonic surprises. Not only do the strings produce a sound between the bridge and the nut but also the segment of string below the bridge and above the nut. And don't forget the wood. There are endless percussive effects to be produced by tapping, slapping, rubbing, and bowing the top, sides, and bridge of the instrument.

Check out Charles Mingus on 1959's "Money Jungle" to hear him pull the string off the side of the fingerboard, adding a delicious "buzz" to the sound of his bass. Listen to Richard Davis, Buell Neidlinger, Peter Kowald, William Parker, Mark Dresser, and others who have continued the quest to expand the low register's sonic palette. Because it's wooden and hollow, your upright bass is full of amazing aural possibilities just waiting to be explored.

TIPS 65 – 77 : EAR TRAINING AND HARMONY

65 BLUES ROOTS

It would be difficult to overstate the profound influence the blues has had on all forms of contemporary music. Throughout the last century, the harmonic core of the blues has colored everything from Charlie Parker and George Gershwin to Beyoncé and the Rolling Stones.

To gain a deeper understanding of the blues spirit, it's important to look at harmonic variations that are the basis for today's music of many genres. Listening to the blues from nearly one hundred years ago, you'll find the harmony is generally lyric driven. The chord progression is not set in stone but rather follows the particular phrasing of the lyric line. Listen to early blues masters like Son House, Blind Lemon Jefferson, Lead Belly, T-Bone Walker, Howlin' Wolf, etc. By exploring the origins of this great musical form, you will gain insights into a vital source of much of today's contemporary music.

Over time, the blues evolved into a somewhat fixed harmonic form. The basic chord structure for the 12-bar blues looks like this:

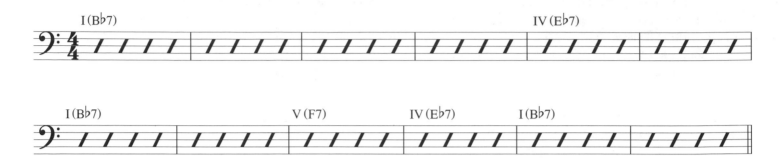

Other blues forms include this 8-bar variation:

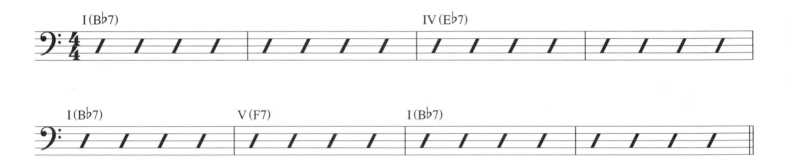

And we have the minor blues, which is also a 12-bar form:

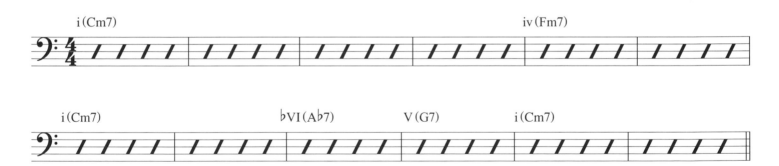

Notice the harmonic relationship indicated by the Roman numeral chord symbols. As you work through these basic blues forms, keep this relationship in mind. This will help to develop a deeper aural understanding of this chord sequence and facilitate the transposition of these blues forms into other keys.

66 FUNCTIONAL EAR TRAINING

There are many avenues into the realm of ear training. Most common are the efforts to identify intervals, chords, melodies, harmonic motion, and basic rhythmic figures. It's important to develop the ability to identify and name qualities of a sound or composite sound. These efforts can be out of context (i.e., simply naming intervals, chords, etc.) or in a musical context (i.e., understanding chord progressions, identifying and imitating song melodies, etc.).

There is another equally important mode of ear training that I like to call *functional ear training*. This is an effort to interpret sound around you and to respond to that sound in an intuitive way. Ultimately, playing in an ensemble is the experience of creating sound and responding to the sound of other musicians. Listening is key! Like a verbal conversation, you want to respond to the ideas of others through further elaboration or by introducing a new but relevant idea. As you develop skills to identify sound, keep in mind that the ability to use these skills effectively in an engaged and responsive way is equally important.

67 THINK "RELATIVE" HARMONY

As you develop a broader understanding of song form and chord structures, it's important to think in terms of "relative" harmony rather than simply the names of the chords. For instance, a song in G major has a tonal center of G—simple enough. The G chord is referred to as the I (one) chord. Each note of the major scale can also function as the root of a chord and is designated like this:

G major (I)
A minor (ii)
B minor (iii)
C major (IV)
D7 (V7)
E minor (vi)
F# diminished (vii dim)

Learn to identify chords in their relationship to the tonic or tonal center of a piece. Complicated chord progressions may require extra attention, as there may be more than one tonal center.

When you see:

Think of the harmonic relationship to the tonic (G major):

Listening more closely to harmony and learning to recognize the harmonic relationship of the chords will yield a deeper insight into the harmonic character of the composition and improve the continuity of the lines you play. Thinking "relative" harmony will also facilitate memorization of songs as well as transposition from one key to another.

68 TRANSCRIBE BASS LINES

Imitating bass lines from your favorite recordings is a valuable learning experience. No doubt some part of your commitment to the upright bass comes from having been completely captivated by the bass line on an early favorite tune. If you haven't already, learn to play along with that bass line exactly as it's played on the recording. Imitate the nuance of the line completely so you can entirely mask the sound of the original recording. Once you have it under your fingers, transcribe it on paper note for note. This process has many benefits and should be a part of your daily practice routine.

First lay out the structure of the line including time and key signatures. Using pencil, enter the rhythmic values of the line, then gradually fill in the pitch for each note. If you're having trouble hearing a particular note, stop the playback just after that note so it will resonate in your ears. If iTunes is your audio player of choice, there is a function in the "Get Info" window that allows you to set the start and end points of the playback. Limit the playback to just four measure segments to focus your efforts and create transcription goals that are realistic. To recap:

1. Lay out the structure of the line. In this case, we have four measures of 4/4 in the key of F major.

2. Listen closely to the rhythmic content and pencil that into the four measures.

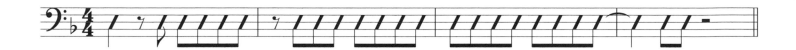

3. Now fill in the pitch value for each note.

TRANSCRIBE TUNES

Another great ear training practice is transcribing entire tunes. Work alone with only your ears and your musical sensibilities (no internet lifeline and no audience participation). Start with a blank page of manuscript, a pencil, and a song that moves you. First determine the basics: What key is it in? What's the time signature? Next listen for structural pieces: How many measures is the intro? Is there a verse? Is there a repeated section with first and second endings? Is there a bridge? Is there some sort of ending or coda? Visualize the entire architecture of the piece.

Since you're a bassist, it may be easiest to begin with the details of the bass line. Transcribe as many notes as possible. If there are some you cannot hear clearly, leave a beat or two blank or write an "x" for the rhythmic value and go on. Continue through the entire tune to get the overall structure down on paper. Then work on the melody. If you first learn to sing the melody, this task will be considerably easier. As with the bass line, leave blank any beats that you cannot clearly identify. Now add the harmony. Listen first for chord types; major, minor or dominant. Work to get the basics in place so you can begin playing along with the recording. As you become more familiar with the tune, fill in the remaining melodic and harmonic details.

If you're planning to play the tune with others, be sure to lay it out on paper the way it sounds when played. If there are four-bar phrases, try to write four bars on each line. Whenever possible, start a new section at the left hand margin of a line. Be clear with repeats, endings, the coda, and all other structural elements so that rehearsal time is not wasted trying to figure out the "road map," but is instead spent practicing the piece.

TRITONE SUBSTITUTIONS

One of the most common devices used in the development of alternate harmonies is the *tritone substitution*. Through this device, it's possible to imply a harmonic idea that gives the impression of a different or more complex harmonic progression without altering the fundamental tonality of the piece.

Typically, dominant chords can easily be substituted with the same chord type whose root is a tritone away—e.g., E7 for B♭7. These two chords have two pitches in common: D and G♯ (A♭), which are the defining 3rd and 7th chord tones.

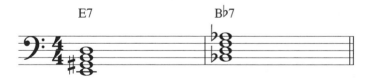

If you lower the 5th of these two chords, you end up with an identical set of pitches.

Experiment with tritone substitutions to:

1. Suggest a tonality other than the original.
2. Create an alternate route from one tonal center (chord) to another.
3. Create harmonic effects that emphasize chord tones other than the root.
4. Support the harmonic direction of a soloist.
5. Suggest harmonic motion where otherwise there is none.

Here's an example using the tritone substitution to create chromatic root movement in a typical ii–V7–I chord progression.

Typical ii–V7–I progression in C:

EXAMPLE 1

| Dm7 | G7 | Cmaj7 | |

With tritone substitution:

EXAMPLE 2

| Dm7 | D♭7 | Cmaj7 | |

Take it one step further from the original harmony by using a tritone substitution for the minor ii chord as well. In this case:

EXAMPLE 3

| A♭m7 | D♭7 | Cmaj7 | |

Experiment with this harmonic device to explore the many variations on simple chord changes that are possible. Work to employ these substitutions discretely so your ideas are effective, meaningful, and spontaneous as you learn to assert your musical identity and lead from the bottom up.

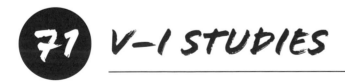

71 V–I STUDIES

The leading contender for "most common harmonic element in Western music" has to be the V–I cadence. The dominant seventh chord on the fifth degree of the major scale resolving to the major chord on the tonic of the major scale is fundamental to all styles of music. Learn to identify this sound and be aware of the different paths that lead to this common harmonic resolution. Notice how often this harmonic unit is found in the tunes that you like to play. Think of this V7–I sound as a harmonic relationship—not simply as a sequence of chord symbols.

Here's a simple study to help establish the V–I sound in your ear. Play the arpeggio of the V7 chord and resolve to the major triad of the I chord as indicated, continuing the pattern through all 12 keys. Listen closely as you play to internalize the sound of this important harmonic element.

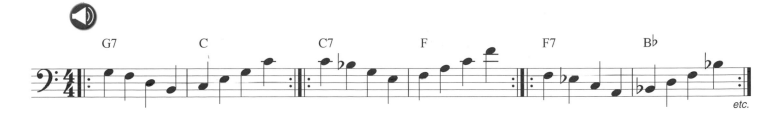

TIPS 72 – 78 : BASS CARE

72 ADJUSTING THE BRIDGE

It's not uncommon for the top of your bass to expand or contract a bit with the change of seasons. Very dry air will cause the wood to lose moisture over time (see tip #75, "Humidifiers"). This can cause the instrument to contract slightly and the action to fall a small amount. Conversely, moist air can cause the instrument to swell and the action to rise. Good bridge adjusters will allow you to keep the strings at a constant height no matter how seasonal changes may affect your bass. Be sure to adjust both sides equally; i.e., if you raise the bridge one complete turn on the E string side, raise the G string side by one complete turn also. This will maintain an even tension on the bridge and the top of your bass.

Bridge Adjusters —

Remember that the height of the strings has a direct impact on the projection of the sound you make. Try raising the action (string height) as your left hand gets stronger and your skills improve. This will strengthen sound projection and increase your dynamic range. Be aware, however, that there is a point of diminishing returns where the action is so high that the bass simply becomes difficult to play while delivering no appreciable difference in sound.

73 BRIDGE ALIGNMENT

The bridge on your bass is not fastened to the instrument in any way. It's held in place by only the tension of the strings. This means that the occasional knock against a chair or a door jam can inadvertently displace the bridge, causing a loss of contact between the feet of the bridge and the top—and thus you'll have a loss of transferred vibration and loss of sound.

If it seems the bridge on your bass has moved slightly, use these guidelines to check its proper position on the top.

- The bridge should be in line with the fingerboard. Look along the line of the fingerboard to see that the bridge is centered.

- Check to see that the feet of the bridge are in line with the inside notches in the *f*-holes.

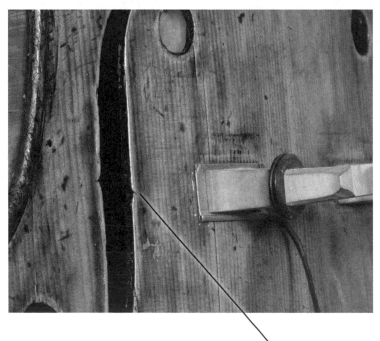

Inside notch

- Check to see that the bridge is standing at 90° to the top of the bass.

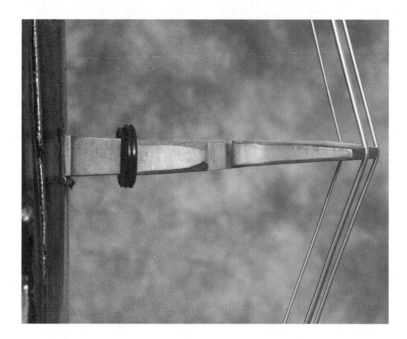

If the bridge is clearly out of place, make adjustments by first loosening the strings about one full turn. Tap lightly on the feet of the bridge to align it with the fingerboard and the ƒ-hole notches. To check the vertical angle, try to slide a small piece of paper underneath the four corners of each foot.

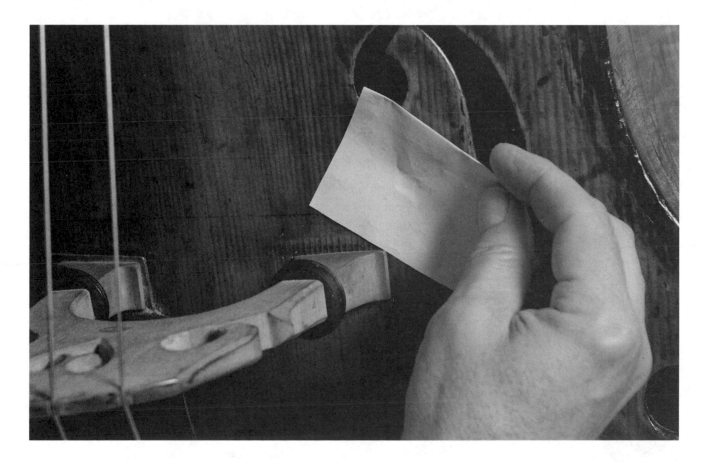

If the paper finds space under any one of the corners, the bridge is probably not exactly vertical. To adjust, very carefully push or tap the top of the bridge toward the tailpiece or toward the fingerboard—depending on which side is not making proper contact. When the paper no longer slips under the corners of the feet, the contact between the bridge and the top is maximized. Tighten the strings and go back to work. For future reference, you may want to make a very small pencil mark on the top to indicate the proper position of the feet of the bridge.

Sometimes a bridge becomes warped over time and will appear to be leaning out of place. If the feet are well seated and there is no space between the bridge and the top, there shouldn't be a loss of sound and the bass will play just fine. At some point, you may want to speak with your luthier about a new bridge.

 ## 74 CAR TALK

Would you leave a wad of cash on the back seat of a locked car? Would you leave a little child in a locked car? Would you leave your bass in a locked car? Hopefully your answer is "no" to all of these questions. First, there's the risk of theft. Even a "cheap" bass is worth hard-earned money that you don't want to lose. Secondly, dramatic changes in temperature can have a damaging impact on your bass. If left in a vehicle for even just a short time, the temperature can rise or fall enough to cause the wood to expand or contract. This sudden temperature change can lead to open seams or cracks, which are costly to repair. So even if it's inconvenient, take the bass out of the car.

 ## 75 HUMIDIFIERS

Do you live in a climate that has low humidity during some part of the year? If so, you should consider some sort of humidifier to add moisture to the air in the room where your bass is kept. Dry air can cause seams to open and can occasionally cause the top or back to crack. Where repairing an open seam is a very routine procedure, the crack repair is more like surgery. It can require the costly removal of the top and sometimes months of "rehabilitation" before the instrument returns to its full potential.

The remedy for overly dry air is fairly simple. Use a humidifier to boost the moisture content of the air in the room where your bass is kept to maintain a healthy instrument. Whether it's the inexpensive warm mist type or the ultrasonic and console models, this little machine is a worthwhile investment. A humidifier will help to maintain the proper moisture content in the wood of your bass. Another humidifying devise called the "Dampit" is made specifically for string instruments and is very effective against damage from dry air. It's essentially a sponge inside a perforated rubber tube that hangs inside the *f*-hole. It can be found at most musical instrument shops or online at your favorite purveyor of bass gear. Whatever device you choose, try to maintain the ideal 40–50% humidity range for a healthy and happy bass.

 ## 76 KEEP IT CLEAN

That's right! Keep your bass clean. Unlike a child that will grow up and learn to look after itself, your bass will forever need your care and attention. It's up to you to keep your bass in good shape by cleaning it regularly. Use a soft, dry cloth to wipe off rosin, sweat, and dust from the body of the instrument. If you're tempted to rub some polish into the finish, definitely avoid anything with silicone or wax, as these compounds can damage the delicate wood varnish on your bass and will reject glue if a repair is ever needed. The fingerboard can withstand a slightly damp cloth if you find a gradual accumulation of sweat and dead skin that's tough to remove. If the build-up is really stubborn, you may have to use just a few drops of rubbing alcohol on super fine steel wool (#0000) to clean down to the ebony. Just be sure to wipe the fingerboard with a soft dry cloth and to replenish the natural oils in the wood with a few drops of mineral oil.

Metal strings can also tolerate a bit of alcohol to clean away the grime. Gut strings can be cleaned and repaired using a drop of mineral oil on a small square of very fine (600 grit) sand paper. If necessary, first use a nail clipper to remove any tiny strands you find separating from the gut string. Finally, remember to wipe your entire instrument with a soft cloth after every practice session, rehearsal and gig. It will look better, the strings will last longer, and it will be easier and more inspiring to play.

77 STAND THE BASS IN THE CORNER

As you've no doubt noticed by now, an upright bass takes up a lot of space. No matter how much room you have, it always seems to be in the middle of everything and exposed to almost constant danger of being bumped, dinged, or scratched. To avoid damage and costly repairs, get in the habit of keeping your bass safe when it's not being played. Leaning it on a chair or table is convenient but probably not entirely secure, as a little slip or mishap could easily send your instrument to the floor. Probably the safest place for your bass when you're not playing it is either standing in a corner with the shoulders leaning against the walls and the bridge facing the corner or laying on its side with the bridge facing away from activity, traffic, and people passing by. Always be sure there is no weight or tension on the neck or scroll. Remember: little precautions can save lots of headaches and expense!

78 WHAT'S THAT SOUND?

The upright bass is a marvel of physics held together by nothing more than clever design, glue, and the tension of the strings. With many delicate parts and constant vibration, there are bound to be things that come loose from time to time. When this happens, it's likely that some alien sound will disrupt the pure bass resonance you're working hard to produce.

To remedy the situation, listen closely to determine whether the noise has a metallic or a wooden source. Metallic sounds most often come from the endpin or from the tuning machines. If the endpin is pushed in completely, try extending it slightly and then tighten the screw. If it has grooves, be sure the screw is well seated in the first groove and not simply on the metal post between grooves. If this doesn't help, check the tuning mechanisms. Hold each tuning peg while playing open strings. If the noise stops while holding one of the tuners, try retuning that string. Sometimes just pushing on the tuner as you tighten it will eliminate the unwanted sound. If the noise seems to be coming from the metal gears, try retuning with slight pressure on the tuning machine. If you can see a place where metal parts are loose, try inserting a tiny piece of paper between them to stop any vibration.

Another possible source of metallic noise is the loose string-ends that can vibrate against the tuning box. This one is easy. Simply twist the string end away from the wood or twist it in some way that holds it firmly in place.

If you use a pickup, there is often an extra length of wire between the transducer and the jack that can vibrate against the top of the bass. Gently loop the wire once and use a rubber band to hold it in place away from the wood of the instrument.

A wooden buzz most often comes from an open seam or a crack in the top or back. This can be more complicated and costly to remedy. Listen closely for the source of the buzz and press lightly on that spot while playing. Often you can see where a seam or crack is open and moves slightly when pressed. Seams are meant to open from time to time as the special glue used to hold the bass together will loosen and crack before the wood of the top and back. The remedy in these cases will require a trip to the luthier for a professionally-crafted repair.

TIPS 79 – 89 : BASS SOLO CONCEPTS

79 BE CONCISE

The Merriam-Webster dictionary defines the word "concise" as "marked by brevity of expression or statement: free from all elaboration and superfluous detail." Work to be concise when a solo opportunity comes your way. Approach your solo space with focus and a disciplined willingness to edit all things superfluous.

Listening to recordings from the pre-LP era, you'll find most arrangements often included an intro, verse, one or two choruses, a solo on some part of the chorus, another chorus, and a coda. All this occurred within about four minutes, which was the time limitation of early recording media. This means that the solo was often no more that eight measures long. On these recordings, musicians like Ben Webster and J.J. Johnson left masterful examples of articulate and well-structured solos that were also very concise.

To explore this concept, learn to develop a mental plan of what you want to say in your solo. Lay out a general shape or tone for your solo. Have some device in mind for a motif you'll develop. As the solo unfolds, keep planning ahead so that your line remains coherent and has a clear direction that leads to an organic conclusion. Be unambiguous about the end point of your solo so your bandmates come in at the appropriate time, and the audience knows it's time to acknowledge your effort with thunderous applause.

80 BREATHE

That's right, breathe. Think like a horn player when you venture into solo territory. Be aware of the length of the phrases that you play and the need to take a breath. Try singing along when you play. This will lead to a more organic quality in your solo line. Be clear with your bandmates that you are not finished with your solo and that you are learning about the use of space.

To learn about pace and balance, practice very consciously taking a breath between each phrase of your solo. This will force you to leave space to separate one "sentence" from the next. The absence of sound is an indispensable element of any well-constructed and balanced musical phrase.

81 COMP FOR ME

It's not every band, nor every tune, that offers solo space for the bassist. So when the opportunity arises, you want to capitalize in every way. Most of the work is to be done by you. Practice different concepts of solo development that will give you a variety of sounds and textures when the spotlight is on you. Be articulate with rhythmic and harmonic execution so that the sound the audience hears is the same as the sound in your mind.

There's also some work to be done by your bandmates. Be direct with the rhythm section to let them know what you like behind your solo. Tell the drummer to lay down a nice groove if that's what you want to hear. Is the guitarist playing too much and filling every space you leave? Make it clear that this is your solo and the space you leave is by design. Be assertive in directing the overall quality of the ensemble sound during your solo. If you like background figures from the horn section, let them know. If necessary, remind them that it is still a bass solo, and their relative volume must be a consideration.

82 DON'T PLAY ON ONE

Here's a simple experiment that will bring quick and significant results. Next time your band gives up a little space for a bass solo, try to avoid beginning any phrase on the first beat of the measure. This effort will force you to think just a little more about the phrase you're about to play and the rhythmic structure of your line. As a practice device, you might even work methodically through the measure, starting a phrase specifically on each successive beat and then on the "and" of each beat as well.

Here's a study you can work on alone. Create a simple phrase and play it starting on each successive eighth note of the measure. Notice the radically different sound that's generated from each of the different placements within the measure.

EXAMPLES 1-4

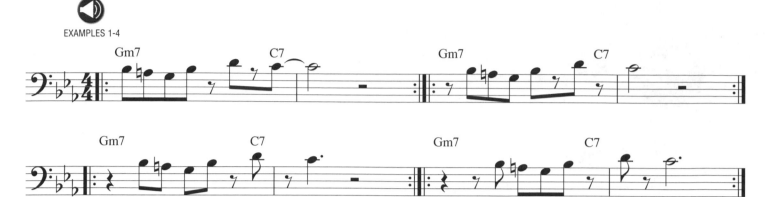

Notice how the line sounds lighter when the rhythm is syncopated and notes fall more often on the "and" of a beat.

83 DON'T PLAY THE ROOT

Here's another idea for developing your solo line: don't play the root of the chord. As a bassist, this might require some discipline. From the day you got your first instrument, you've been the harmonic anchor for every band you've played in by focusing on the root of each chord. Emphasizing the root is fundamental to a solid bass line in all styles of music. However, if it's a solo line you're working on, "fuggedaboutit." Consciously avoid the root tone and start each phrase on other chord tones instead. Just as in tip #82 ("Don't Play on One"), you'll achieve real progress by incorporating this simple concept into your solo practice.

84 LEARN THE MELODY

There are many devices we can use to develop a strong and relevant solo line. But before thinking about rhythmic variation, harmonic invention, and more sophisticated concepts, you should learn the melody. This will provide a reliable connection to the tune you're playing no matter where your solo may take you. Be sure to get the notes right from beginning to end before you experiment with more adventurous interpretations. Listen to original recordings to be sure you're starting with accurate information (melody and harmony).

As you get the right notes under your fingers, try this exercise to strengthen your understanding of the melody and to develop a "connected" solo line: play through the tune, alternating between the original melody and an improvised line. For example, play the first two measures of the melody, then two measures of solo, two more measures of the melody, two measures of solo, etc. Work to construct a line that leads organically from one section to the next.

85 LEARN LYRICS

Think of lyrics as a facet of a song that is inseparable from the whole. Knowing the lyrics helps you to better understand the character of the song and inform your interpretation of the melody. Knowing the stressed words and syllables in a text will guide the emphasis and shape you bring to a melodic line. Learning lyrics also helps to keep track of the harmonic form. A tune with an AABA harmonic structure has different text for each A section, effectively making it ABCD. Knowing lyrics is also a reminder to tell a story in your solo and help connect your line to the original melody.

86 THINK "MOTIF" IN YOUR SOLO

Human beings seem to love a narrative. We're always looking for a connection between linear events that follow each other in real time. Try to create this narrative quality in your solo line with elements of a good story: a beginning, middle, and end, character (motif) development, humor, irony, etc.

Think about how the phrases of your solo relate to each other. You may play a series of good ideas but have no connecting element. Imagine taking a page from five well-written novels and reading them together as one story. Each page alone may be interesting, but together they don't make sense. Work to connect each phrase, section, and chorus of your solo to create a single arc from beginning to end.

Here's a study to help you develop a stronger sense of motif in your playing. Play through a basic 12-bar blues form using a simple melodic motif carefully altered to accommodate the harmonic changes. Be disciplined enough to continue with the same motif throughout the entire chorus. Work to extend the gradual development of your motif over two or three choruses—not two or three measures. In the following example, the motif is a simple three-note element that is altered just enough to fit the changing harmony. Notice how simple rhythmic variations add interest and complexity to an otherwise mundane solo idea.

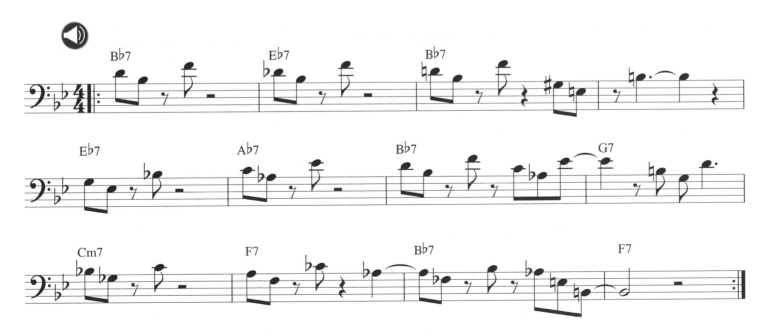

⟨87⟩ RHYTHMIC VARIATION

Along with dynamic range, rhythmic variation is something you can add to your solo lines starting today. It just takes concentration and a little practice. Bass lines by nature are often repetitive, functioning within the rhythm section and focused primarily on a solid and consistent pulse or groove. Playing a rhythmic sequence over and over in this supportive role can be musically appropriate and effective. When the solo spot arrives, however, greater rhythmic diversity is a must and will add interest and substance to your efforts. In practice sessions, work very consciously to alter the rhythmic content of the solo lines you play, even if this seems to lead to a dead end from time to time.

Here's a study to kick start your experiments in rhythmic variation. Play through the B♭ major scale using the various rhythms shown below. Be sure to make all rhythms precise. Notice the subtle yet critical difference between half-note triplets and dotted quarter notes. Use a metronome when playing this exercise to maintain a constant pulse, starting at a tempo where you can comfortably execute the fastest notes (eighth-note triplets). When you get the hang of it, try these methodical rhythmic variations with other scales. Add another level of complexity by including rests in this study.

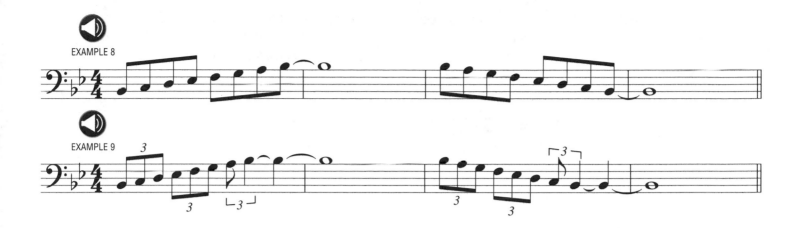

EXAMPLE 8

EXAMPLE 9

88 IN TIME/OUT OF TIME

Here's a study to help you internalize a more stable sense of pulse while you develop interest and variation in your solo phrasing. Experiment with playing a solo line that alternates between being in time and out of time. Using a tune that you know well as the vehicle, play a four-measure phrase using very clear and concise rhythmic devices. Then play four measures with a very free rhythmic sense, floating over the changes with no apparent concern for the beat. Continue this rhythmic model through the entire form of the tune.

Work to make the distinction evident and sensible. Create a strong contrast between strict time measures and free time measures. Listen to Miles Davis' solo on the original recording of "Milestones." You'll hear a masterful application of this concept, where the A section of his solo is locked in with the rhythm section and the B section is "floating" over the beat. As you gain control of this dynamic experiment, try making your phrases longer and the distinction between playing in time and out of time more subtle.

89 UP-TEMPO SOLOS

No doubt you've struggled at some point with playing a solo on up-tempo songs. Sometimes just sustaining a solid and energized bass line can be enough of a challenge, and then the band looks over to see if you want to take a solo chorus or two. The next time this happens, just nod your head and dive in. There are simple strategies for executing an effective solo even if your monster chops are still a work in progress.

As you work to develop the articulation and mental process required to string together a line of blistering eighth notes, learn to simply imply a fast tempo. In other words, think fast, but play slowly. Experiment with playing an eighth-note line in shorter phrases with a few beats of rest in between. This will allow time to visualize the next phrase and to get your hand in position to play it. Structure your ideas around some clear motivic element to give continuity to the larger shape of the solo. Let the rhythm section carry the pulse forward while you interject shorter melodic lines that you can handle.

Another approach is to think in longer melodic phrases rather than short, rhythmically-driven phrases. Play more quarter notes and half notes to create a line with a broader arc that bridges larger harmonic segments. Be creative with a rhythmic structure that emphasizes longer notes through the measure and across the bar line.

TIPS 90 – 101 : OTHER ADVICE

90 AMP UP

Are you regularly using an amplifier when you play? Try placing it on a chair or footstool for a more articulate sound. If the amp is sitting on the floor, the vibration of the speaker can transfer to the floor and create a low-frequency rumble; a boomy wash that diffuses the focused acoustic sound of your bass. With the amp raised off the floor, the transfer of sound is reduced, the amplified sound is cleaner, and everyone will hear more detail in the notes you play.

Consider using a microphone as an alternative to a pickup when there's a need to amplify your bass. There are several clip-on mics currently available designed specifically for the acoustic bass as well as stand-alone mics that deliver a very natural quality sound. These mics are typically positioned in front of the *f*-hole (G-string side) and sometimes wrapped in a hand towel and slid under the bridge or wedged behind the tailpiece. The results will vary depending on the type of mic you use and the unique sonic characteristics of your bass. Experiment with different mic placement options to find the amplified sound you find most true to your instrument.

91 TEACH WHAT YOU KNOW

As you become proficient at playing the upright bass, consider teaching a bit. Just as there is always someone who knows more than you, there is also someone who knows less. Take the time to help a classmate or other fellow bassist in need of some practice ideas. This exchange is not only helpful to the student but also brings focus and definition to your own thoughts. Verbalizing what you think about when you practice and play can be a great learning experience.

92 SAVE YOUR BACK

Playing and transporting the upright bass is a very physical activity. Even with attention to proper posture and the use of transportation aids, chronic back problems often arise. Fortunately, there are steps you can take to thwart this common bass player ailment.

Think first about prevention. Practice good posture when you play, take breaks to give your back a rest and exercise regularly. This can include just about anything that gets your body moving: walking, running, swimming (probably the best exercise for maintaining a healthy back), weight training, sports, etc. Any regular workout activity is not only good for your back but also good for your overall physical, mental, and emotional well-being. Along with exercise, stretching is another critical element in your preventive care practice. A quick online search will lead to many valuable suggestions for lower back stretches. Experiment with a variety of options and find a few stretches that work best for you.

If you should develop back problems, seek the advice of a professional, such as a practitioner of chiropractic, yoga, Alexander Technique, Pilates, or other discipline that helps to realign and strengthen the entire body and bring relief of back pain. It's never too soon to start thinking about maintaining a healthy back.

93 MEMORIZING REPERTOIRE

The memory is like a muscle that you can strengthen through exercise. With regular practice, you can increase your ability to memorize music and build your repertoire; a critical quality of a well-rounded musician. To do this, you must consciously challenge yourself to remember melodies and chord changes without the need for written music.

At your next rehearsal, try turning the written music over after the third or fourth time playing through it. Starting out, try only eight measures at a time. Two important processes are engaged. First, your mind must look for a thread back to the last time your eyes were on the music to recall the right notes and chords for those eight measures. This strengthens the memory process. Second, your ears become more engaged to compare your memory to the sounds of the chordal instruments. If no neuron path takes you back to the correct information in your mind, your ears are then responsible to identify the evolving harmony and to guide the direction of your bass line.

You want to gradually conceive of larger harmonic units as unique sounds rather than the sum of smaller elements. Learn to mentally organize music into distinct structural segments and build an inventory of common harmonic forms and predictable root movements. When learning basic harmony, it's common to think of a chord as a combination of intervals. For example, G7 indicates the root, G, the major 3rd, B, the 5th, D, and the ♭7th, F. Through your ear training efforts, it's common for this chord symbol to gradually imply a composite sound, G7, and to hear this as a unique harmonic element rather than the sum of three different intervals. Likewise, to more easily memorize a song as a set of chord changes, begin to listen for those elements that you can identify as unique. A ii–V7–I progression, for example, is a simple harmonic element and one that can easily assume the quality of a distinct sound. Work to expand this approach to include longer passages, such as the first eight measures of the song "Autumn Leaves." Committing music to memory becomes easier as you bundle a series of chord changes into larger harmonic chunks.

94 FIRST REHEARSAL WITH A NEW BAND

Have you ever been a little nervous about playing with a new band? Here are some things to remember to help make this experience go smoothly:

- **Be on time**. There's nothing that says "I'm not terribly interested" like a late arrival for the first rehearsal.

- **Bring all necessary equipment**. If you think you might need items such as a music stand, stool, or an amp, be sure to have them on hand. Although breaking strings is a rarity, it never hurts to have an extra set in your bass case.

- **Listen to all available recordings of the new band days (or even weeks) before the rehearsal**. Not only does this prepare you for the music you're about to play, but it reflects a serious attitude about this new situation and a willingness to do what's necessary to get up to speed.

- **When the playing begins, the first order of business is to hook up with the drummer (see tip #64, "Who's Your Drummer?").** Quickly come to a consensus about the pulse and feel the rhythm section will project. Don't hesitate to defer to the drummer of the band while you discreetly assert your own musical identity.

- **If the group has a leader (as most do), keep your eyes and ears on him/her to follow inevitable cues.** This concerns not just directions in the chart but things like phrasing, dynamics, intonation, and balance. You want to make the leader and other musicians feel comfortable with your musical contribution.

- **Be sure to focus on the soloist and be willing to play a supportive role.** The rhythm section is meant to support and encourage the soloist.

95 PLAY EVERY CHANCE YOU GET

That's right, play every chance you get! Play with a community orchestra, bluegrass band, local musical production, gospel group, the jazz players in town, etc. While some playing opportunities will be more productive than others, just making the effort is critical. Even if this involves playing music that is not exactly your cup of tea, at least you have the bass in your hands and your instrumental skills are getting some exercise. You may even grow to enjoy playing musical styles that you never considered inspiring. The object is to play as much as possible. And while you're out there just playing the bass, you're developing the indispensable network that might bring bigger and better opportunities.

96 TRAVEL TIPS

Traveling with an upright bass is not a simple matter. First, buy a quality padded soft case to protect your instrument no matter how you plan to get around. Always be aware of the scroll and the bridge, as these are the two places that protrude the most and are most likely to take a hit.

If the bass is lying down in the back of a station wagon or van, be sure to support the shoulders in some way so that the weight of the instrument is not resting on the neck or scroll. The tension of the strings puts 250–300 pounds of pressure on the neck and top. Adding to this, the weight of the instrument can potentially crack the neck block or top. Use a bungee cord attached to a secure part of the car or some padding to keep your bass from sliding around. If you're driving a sedan, you can put the bass in the front passenger-side seat. First, slide the seat away from the dashboard and recline it all the way back **[Fig. 3]**. The bass enters neck first with the bridge facing the steering wheel. Carefully lift your bass over the headrest of the driver's seat and toward the back window until the body comes to rest easily on its side in the front passenger's seat [**Fig. 4**].

Fig. 3

Fig. 4

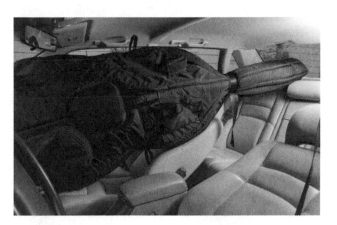

Riding in a taxi with a bass can be an adventure. First and foremost, be polite to your driver. They have (and often exercise) the right to refuse your fare. As previously mentioned, the front seat can work but many drivers are not willing to yield this space. The best option is to find a minivan or SUV-style taxi that has space for your instrument behind the back seats or over a back seat that folds down. As a last resort, slide the bass across the back seat, end-pin first, and climb in under the neck with the scroll extending out the open window. In this dire situation, be sure to tell the driver that his/her generous tip is directly related to the condition of the piece of wood protruding from the back window.

When traveling by train, the best place for your bass is in the seat next to you. Have a bungee cord available to secure the neck to the overhead rack or coat hook. If you must leave your bass in a luggage area away from your seat, find a way to secure it to some part of the train and be especially cautious at station stops. Besides the obvious security risk, you want to be sure other travelers don't see your fragile instrument as just another piece of luggage and toss a loaded suitcase on top of it.

Flying with a bass has become increasingly difficult. There are excellent flight cases on the market that can protect your bass in transit and are worth the investment if you plan to be touring internationally. It is critical, however, that you speak with an agent for the airline to confirm your special needs and to be sure that your instrument is acceptable as checked baggage. Many airlines will insist the instrument be shipped as cargo, which requires additional time and organization.

Another option in the new millennium is the modern travel bass. With historical precedent going back more than two hundred years, some basses are designed to come apart! The big advantage here is a bolted neck that can be removed and reassembled in just minutes. These instruments fit inside a relatively small flight case that meets normal airline regulations.

97 *POSTURE*

If you typically stand while playing the upright bass, your posture can greatly impact your ability to play and your long-term health as well. Your upper body should remain over your hips as much as possible with your weight distributed evenly between both legs. Allow some gentle movement from side to side like a tennis player about to receive a serve. Stay relaxed and flexible with your knees slightly bent and not locked into place.

Work to maintain this upright posture even when playing in thumb position. Resist the inclination to hunch over the shoulders of the instrument like Quasimodo. Learn to balance your bass against your belly so there's no need to rest the neck on your shoulder as you move up the fingerboard. Your elbow should be above the shoulder of the bass with your hand above the strings. This will offer greater flexibility of motion into and out of thumb position, making your lines more fluid and articulate.

Bad posture

Good posture

 ## PROTECT YOUR INVESTMENT

It's important to view your instrument as an investment no matter what its value. Unlike most material things we buy, the value of a good string instrument will gradually appreciate over time. When we walk out the door of the luthier carrying a "new" bass, its value does not suddenly decrease. This is very different than buying a new car or a new pair of shoes. To protect the investment you've made, consider purchasing musical instrument insurance. There are many reputable companies that offer an affordable policy alone or as an add-on to a homeowner's/renter's policy.